MOM'S EVERYTHING BOOK
FOR DAUGHTERS

Other Books in This Series

MOM'S EVERYTHING BOOK FOR DAUGHTERS

• practical ideas for a quality relationship •

WOMEN OF FAITH℠

BECKY FREEMAN

ZONDERVAN®

ZONDERVAN.com/
AUTHORTRACKER
follow your favorite authors

To my daughter, Rachel, who lights up my life with her compassion, joy, and beautiful way of being.

◼ ZONDERVAN®

Mom's Everything Book for Daughters
Copyright © 2002 by Becky Freeman and Women of Faith, Inc.

Requests for information should be addressed to:

Zondervan, *Grand Rapids, Michigan* 49530

Library of Congress Cataloging-in-Publication Data

Freeman, Becky, 1959-
    Mom's everything book for daughters : practical ideas for a quality relationship /
by Becky Freeman.
       p.   cm.
    Includes bibliographical references.
    ISBN-10: 0-310-24294-0
    ISBN-13: 978-0-310-24294-9
    1. Mothers and daughters. 2. Mothers—Conduct of life. 3. Mothers—Life skills
guides. 4. Daughters—Psychology. I. Title.
HQ755.85 .F754 2002
306.874'3—dc21
                                                               2002008235

Published in association with the literary agency of Alive Communications, Inc., 7680 Goddard Street, Suite 200, Colorado Springs, CO 80920.

Interior design by Todd Sprague

Printed in the United States of America

Contents

How to Read This Book

This is a book to help you be a *real* mother to your equally *real* daughter. It is a collection of practical ideas you can use to create memorable moments, one after another, with your child. And don't worry, Martha Stewart doesn't live at my house—in fact, she probably wouldn't even want to visit. So the ideas will be quick and do-able. I'll include suggestions for those in-the-car conversations, hands-on fun, with other great resources to explore should you want to inquire more.

Think of this book as Mom and Daughter Idea Popcorn. Open it up and reach in for a motivational snack, an "Ah-ha" moment, something to do when it is raining outside and your daughter is whining, "I'm so bored."

Some of these ideas, if you do them, will produce actual real-life moments. And some of these moments will sink deep into your daughter's memory.

And these memories, strung together like charms on a bracelet, are part of what will bond you together as mother and daughter for all eternity.

What could be more important?

A Song in Your Heart

A girlfriend of mine from childhood, Lou Ann Lee, is now all grown up with a daughter of her own. Lou Ann is an incredible songwriter, musician, and a full-time worship leader for a large church in California. (I remember when "Little Lou Ann" was about nine years old, playing songs in our little small-town church in Texas. Another reminder that little girls are seedlings that flower into wonderful women of God.) She allowed me to reprint the following from a song she wrote, a duet that she and her daughter, Brianna, sang together at church. I hope the lyrics bless you as they've blessed me. I cannot think of a better place to begin this book than to start with a reminder of what's most important in our busy lives.

You Are My Ministry

Verse 1: Others might need me but you come first.
I'd swim across the ocean, I'd walk across this earth,
just to show you how much your worth.
You are my ministry.

Chorus: You are my ministry. You mean the world to me.
Out of all of the girls in the whole wide world, you are most
precious to me. You are my ministry.

Verse 2: At night when we pray and I hold your hand,
I know the Father's watching and unfolding His plan.
And it is an honor to be right where I am,
for you are my ministry.

Chorus

Bridge: Darling, you light up my life, you bring me joy on my
        darkest night.
Having you shows me what matters in life, and that's to slow
        down, unwind,
wrap my arms around the precious daughter of mine.

Verse 3: (Daughter sings) I know that there will come a day,
when you will grow old but, Mommy, don't be afraid.
I'll take care of you like you took care of me.
For you are my ministry.[1]

---

[1] For information on this song or Lou Ann's ministry in music or a copy
of this song on CD, email her at cedriclee@jps.net.

chapter one

The Wind Beneath Her Wings or The Gum Beneath Her Shoes?

Bonding with Your Daughter for a Lifetime

I t was subtle at first, like a gauze curtain between us, this growing distance. Then one afternoon I looked at my beautiful daughter, age thirteen, and her eyes darted away from me, almost on instinct.

"What's wrong?" I asked her. "Why have you been so snippy with me lately? Is it PMS? Something I've said?"

"Like you really care," she mumbled and sulked upstairs to her bedroom.

The gauze between us transformed into a full-fledged brick wall.

Well, not as long as I'm still the mother, I thought to myself. I would find a way to chisel through this hard silence.

I followed Rachel up the steps, then following some wacky maternal impulse, I climbed into her bed, pulled her pink-and-silver comforter up around my chin and declared, "I'm having a tuck-in until you talk to me and tell me what's been bothering you."

"What's a tuck-in?" she asked, her eyes wide.

"I'm going to stay tucked in your bed—for *days* if that's what it takes—until we talk."

Slowly, she grinned, eventually succumbing to the undertow of laughter. A good sign. Then in the midst of the laughter, her voice suddenly broke, and she was crying.

Also a good sign. I love the line from the great mother-daughter movie *Steel Magnolias:* "Laughter through tears is my favorite emotion."

Gingerly, Rachel sat down beside me, pushed away a damp strawberry blond curl from her cheek, and said, "Mom, look: When you are traveling on the weekends and speaking at these ladies' retreats, you are different when you come home. It's like you're on a parade float, waving at us—like we are a crowd on the sidelines. But you don't really see me; you don't *hear* me. You just say what you have to say to sound like a good mother and pretend you are interested. But you aren't really here. You are somewhere else in your mind."

Chick Chat

You Oughta Be in Pictures

Plan a time to look over baby pictures and girlhood pictures together. Memories will naturally evoke some great connective conversation. Bring out some of your daughter's old baby clothes or cards you received at her baby shower.

Ouch! The truth hurts. Especially when it comes from your pubescent offspring.

"Rachel," I said, sitting up in her bed, reaching out and pulling her close to my heart, "you're right. I have to admit it is so hard for me to transition from being a speaker at a retreat and bonding with all these women who live miles away, and then suddenly—*zap!*—get off the plane, and back into my role here as wife and mom and homemaker. It's sort of like when you go to church camp and it takes you a couple of days to get used to being our kid again."

"I know," she said tearfully.

"But you know what?" I said. "I really miss you guys. No one in the world is as important to me as you and your brothers and your dad. This is where my real life begins and ends, right here, in this house. All I love most lives under this roof. And my traveling to minister, obviously, isn't working well if my first love— this family—isn't feeling so loved after all. So we need to make some changes around here."

"Like what?" she asked.

"Like, I'm going to cut my travel down to one weekend a month until all of you kids are out of high school. And I'm not going to travel in the summer at all, or between Thanksgiving and New Year's. That will be Sacred Family Time. How's that sound?"

"Better."

"It sounds better to me too. I love you so much, Rachel Praise."

"I love you too, Mom," she said, smiling again. The bricks were tumbling down; we could see each other clearly again. She rose from the bed, tugged at the pillow behind me, and grinned. "Now, would you get out of my bed?"

Life as a mother is nothing more than a series of moments with our children, one after the other. It is not so important that we do all these moments perfectly, because, in truth, we cannot. And life itself is a poignant mixture of joy and woe, moments of laughing aloud together at a movie, and moments of yelling and slamming doors.

Most of us parents who have been at it awhile admit that we mostly wing it from day to day. We are a learn-as-you-go lot. And that is fine, because parenting is 99 percent instinct and common sense as long as you throw in big hunks of love, affection, prayer, discipline, and a willingness to yelp for help when you are stuck.

What matters most is that we tend to our relationships with our children, paying attention to them, remembering their importance in the grand scheme of our life here on earth, and into eternity. Not because some parenting book tells you it is what you have to do to be a model citizen. But because loving relationships in families are what make life on this planet rich with meaning and joy. It is living as God designed us to live.

I see brilliant orange and golden yellow leaves, dripping with fresh rain, outside my office window this morning. Thanksgiving was just a few days ago. On that day of blessing, I couldn't help thinking of the hilarious idiosyncrasies, the soap-opera-style dramas, that go on behind the beautiful turkey and dressing feasts across our nation. What leaves me stunned with gratitude is not that families are so marvelous, but that *they are such a mess* and—wonder of wonders—we still love, put up with, and pray good things for one another! Perhaps the family relationship most fraught with emotion is that special bond (or sometimes brick wall) between mother and daughter.

Bonding Glue for the Two of You

When I chat with mothers of young daughters, one of the most common fears they share is that the bond they feel with their child now will somehow blow up and dissolve when their daughter hits the stormy teenage years. Best-selling books with titles like *When You and Your Mother Can't Be Friends* or the infamous *Mommy Dearest* can make any woman feel uneasy about what evils may lurk ahead for their relationship with their daughter—beyond Pablum and puberty.

Certainly, the growing independence of the teen years poses challenges, but these fears of mother-daughter relationships inevitably going awry are simply unfounded. For example, in a recent collaborative survey between *Ladies' Home Journal* and *Seventeen* magazine, there were surprising discoveries about mothers and daughters, many of them incredibly reassuring. According to the popular stereotype, you would assume mothers and their teen daughters are locked in near-constant combat. Good news: the reality is much more rosy. A whopping 95 percent of moms say they feel close to their daughters, with 42 percent claiming to be best friends. The daughters responded similarly—the vast majority reporting that their mothers are supportive and that they are true friends. In addition, most mothers today (three out of four) feel they are much closer to their daughters than they were to their mothers.

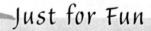

Just for Fun

Buy a set of refrigerator word magnets that allows you to make up funny or heartwarming personalized messages between the two of you. You never know what you might find on your "refrigerator marquee" as you go for that midnight snack!

What to Do, What to Do?

Accepting that this mother-daughter friendship is based on many good moments together through the years, what are the ideal ways to spend quality time bonding with your daughter?

Well, here is where the moms and daughters had slightly different opinions, according to the survey. Both enjoyed sitting around and talking, going to lunch and a movie, and shopping together. However, the moms were really big on "sitting and talking" time, while not too surprisingly, the daughters enjoyed shopping the most—especially if mom was footing the bill! One of the things Rachel and I have enjoyed most together through the years is occasionally watching a Girls Only Saturday afternoon video, often accompanied by the weekly activity of folding mounds of laundry. Though some of my classic movies or musicals seemed a little old-fashioned to my daughter at first, I good-naturedly ignored her, stuck in the video, and smiled. "Just humor your old mother, okay?" (My favorite movies to watch with girls ages eight to twelve are listed on the next page.)

In spite of some of Rachel's initial protests to "old-timey movies," she soon found herself as caught up in the story, the costumes, and the music as I once was—and I've often caught her watching again *My Fair Lady* or *Seven Brides for Seven Brothers* or humming a singable tune in spite of herself.

A Long Line of Love

Although we love it when our daughters earn good grades or show special talents, the majority of mothers, according to this survey, are most proud of their daughters when they observe them performing good deeds. This morning my daughter was sifting through the mail and came across a letter from World Vision, where we give a small monthly financial pledge to help a young girl from El Salvador. (I always keep Damaris Iveth's picture and letters on our fridge. Our family loves watching her "grow up" through these yearly photos.)

"Mom," Rachel asked, "are we going to send Damaris something special for Easter? We need to, you know." And my heart

Rave Reviews

Becky's Favorite Mother–Daughter Chick Flick Picks

Thanks to several of my mother-of-daughter friends for their suggestions below as well.

Anne of Green Gables
Bringing Up Baby
Christmas in Connecticut (the old version)
Emma
Father of the Bride
Fiddler on the Roof
Gone with the Wind
It's a Wonderful Life
The King and I
Little Women
The Man from Snowy River
Mary Poppins
Miracle on 34th Street
The Music Man
My Fair Lady
Oklahoma!
Persuasion
Princess Bride
Princess Caraboo
Princess Diaries
Sabrina (with Audrey Hepburn)
Sense and Sensibility
Seven Brides for Seven Brothers
Shirley Temple movies
Singing in the Rain
The Sound of Music
South Pacific
Anything by Rogers and Hammerstein—timeless and toe-tapping!

warmed. So much of compassion is caught rather than taught, and one way to build in bonding time with your daughter is to be an example of kindness in your own world. She will take note and will follow your lead.

For example, I have a special place in my heart for children and have always enjoyed wee ones. To my delight, I've observed how my own daughter automatically reaches out to young ones with tenderness and warmth and ease. Rachel began babysitting a young toddler and his baby twin siblings down the street, starting from the time she was eleven years old—apprenticing by working alongside the young mother, changing countless preemie diapers and reading a stack of Dr. Suess books to the big brother who hungered for special attention as well. This Christmas Rachel also participated in a program at Wal-Mart where several teens arrived early to take a young, underprivileged child on a shopping spree. Later the teens decided on their own to throw these same children a wonderful Christmas party.

In thinking back at my own legacy of female benevolence, I realize that my tender heart might have been born of nurture, rather than nature, as well. My mother often invited a mentally challenged, newly adopted little girl named Sunny in our home for "special visits" to give the child's exhausted mother a much-needed break. Mom always kept—and still does—a closet full of toys for anyone who might visit and bring little ones with them. She adored rocking the newborns in the church nursery, and grew up watching her own mother, my "Nonnie," take delight in caring for babies.

Nine Ways to Make Your Daughter Feel Loved

Here are some other ways to build mother-daughter connections:

1. **Give her the gift of your presence.** Listen with focused attention, look in her eyes, sit down, slow down. Touch her in motherly ways: stroke her hair, rub her arm, hug her.

2. **Speak to her with respect and kindness.** If you are stuck in a rut of being cranky with your kids, try the mental trick of treating them like guests in your home for day. My mom used to say, "Treat your guests like family, and your family like guests."

3. **Encourage her efforts with enthusiasm.** Let her know she has her own private cheerleader to count on at home. Convey that it is her courage to *try* new things that makes you most proud, whatever the results.

4. **Seek first to understand your daughter's point of view—** and let her know you really hear her, before you express your own opinion. This is one of most profound and helpful "Habits of Highly Effective Families" as taught by Stephen Covey. It is also one of the most challenging habits to implement!

5. **Answer her honest questions with honest answers.** "Good question! I don't know, but I'll try to find out" is always appropriate.

6. **Say yes whenever you possibly can.** Reserve no for when it is necessary.

7. **Ask her opinion.** Girls love giving advice. Or even better yet, share something you've learned *from her.* You can almost see the self-esteem rising in a child's face when you say something as simple as, "Come taste this soup, would you, Babe? You are such a naturally good cook. What do you think? More salt? More garlic?"

8. **Allow your daughter to feel *any feelings* she may have.** In fact, if there is such a thing as a functional family (most of us can only hope for fairly functional)—the common denominator is that all feelings are allowed and able

to be expressed. However, you do have to teach her ways she can express those feelings, and ways she cannot, without damaging relationships.

9. **Let her cry, and don't be afraid to cry with her too.** Part of teaching empathy and tolerance is to allow for "the crankies" in your family now and then. If it becomes habitual, you'll have to take a different turn, but everyone has bad days, and you will want her to be understanding when you are frustrated with life too. Maybe you can have a family Teddy Bear that is passed to the person most in need of some extra love and cuddling on a particularly trying day.

You will probably be surprised one day when you ask your daughter what she remembers most about your times together. Most often it isn't the grand, planned mother-daughter occasions—but the small kindnesses, the little notes on her pillow or in her lunch box, the "folding laundry and watching a video" times of coziness and warmth and fun that bind her heart, forever, to yours.

God, Mom, and Me

Read Proverbs 31:10–31 together in an easy-to-understand translation (*The Living Bible* and *The Message* are great). Working together through this passage, make a list of all the qualities of a virtuous woman. (For example: speaks kindly, isn't lazy, helps the poor . . .)

Look up the word *virtuous* in a dictionary together and share its meaning.

Then have your daughter divide a big piece of paper or a poster board into four to eight sections. At the top write, "A Virtuous Woman is . . ." and then in each square write one of the qualities your daughter likes best from this passage. Illustrate that quality or cut and paste pictures from magazines of women or girls illustrating the virtue. She may want to hang this in her room somewhere as a reminder of the kind of person she most wants to be.

Beauty At What Price?

Fostering a Positive Body Image

I picked up the teen girl magazine Rachel had ordered through the mail—with my permission, for her birthday—and began thumbing through it. Within minutes, I had learned more than I ever wanted to know. When did teenage magazines turn into sex manuals? When did young models start looking street-urchin thin?

It was time for a Mother-Daughter Porch Swing Talk.

Once I had Rachel settled on the back porch swing near me, I opened the magazine and read the table of contents aloud. "Oh this is great. Listen here: 'How to Attract Guys with Six Sexy Moves,' 'Flirting 101,' 'Be a Size 5 in 4 days!'"

Rachel wriggled uncomfortably. "Mom, this was my birthday present. You said I could order it."

"But, Honey, I didn't realize what was inside the pages. These just aren't the sort of messages I want you to hear. God made you beautiful exactly the way you are. And the right guy will be attracted to your inner and outer beauty—at the right time—without any premeditated 'sexy moves.'"

"Moomm," she wailed. "I don't take this stuff seriously."

"Okay, let me ask you something. When you read through this magazine do you find yourself thinking, 'Boy, I wish I looked like her,' and then thinking of all the things about yourself that aren't quite good enough or pretty enough or skinny enough? Be honest."

"Well, yeah, sometimes. How did you know?"

"Because I'm female, and I fight those same kind of self-defeating thoughts like every other woman on the planet. But let me tell you a story about something that happened to me one day that helped me look at myself in a brand-new way."

Rachel rolled her eyes as if to say, "Here goes the story-with-a-moral routine." But I am a mother so I pressed on.

"One day I went into a store to buy a pack of gum and when I came out, this huge man wearing a flannel suit, suspenders, and a funny hat was standing on the sidewalk. He said, 'You sure are pretty, ma'am.' Well, I always take compliments wherever I can get them so I said, 'Thank you,' and headed to Grandy's for breakfast. As I started to order, I heard this familiar voice behind me. It was that big man—he had followed me to the restaurant! Now I need to tell you that this guy obviously didn't have both oars in the water—he was mentally slow. He asked if he could buy me a cup of coffee, and I told him I was sorry but he couldn't because I was married. He looked as though he'd been kicked in the stomach, so hurt was the look on his face. And then he looked at me wistfully and said the oddest thing, especially since we had never seen each other before. He said, 'I just never met a woman quite like you.'"

"How weird!" Rachel said, obviously paying attention now.

"I know. But once I realized the man was harmless, I couldn't get his comment out of my head. I had been comparing myself a lot to other women, always feeling chubbier, dumber, less organized, that kind of thing. When this guy said he'd never met a woman quite like me, I realized, perhaps for the very first time, that he was absolutely right. There isn't another woman out there quite like me. I'm uniquely made by God!"

Rachel smiled. "Boy, you can say that again."

I laughed. "And you know what?" I asked as I slipped my arm around her shoulder. "There's not another girl out there in the whole wide world exactly like you. You are fantastic—

Chick Chat

Matter-of-factly talk to your daughter about anorexia and bulimia and the often tragic results.

What to say? Here's a simple explanation that might be helpful:

Being a preteen girl can be tough, and sometimes girls who are healthy try to lose weight even though they don't need to. You may feel a lot of pressure to look a certain way. Acting on this pressure may lead to eating disorders like anorexia nervosa or bulimia nervosa.

Anorexia nervosa is a form of self-starvation where a person does not eat enough food to keep healthy and does not maintain a healthy weight.

Bulimia nervosa is when a person eats a lot of food and then vomits or uses other methods, such as fasting or exercising too much, to avoid gaining weight after overeating.

If you ever start thinking that you want to look and feel better, talk to me, and we can work together as a team to make small changes in our family eating and physical activity habits—without going overboard. Okay?

just the way you are. I wouldn't change a thing. So what do ya say we cancel this stupid magazine subscription and take the money we save and go shopping for a new pair of jeans for your birthday instead. Deal?"

"Okay," she agreed. "It's a deal. But can I get my ears pierced instead of the jeans?"

I raised my eyebrows.

"Remember how there's not another girl out there quite like me," she purred. "And remember it's *my* birthday present."

What's a mother to say?

Within two hours we were at the mall. Rachel was squeezing back tears and holding my hand—and sporting two red ear lobes with shiny silver studs.

Media Blitzed

Experiments show that we become significantly more dissatisfied with our own appearance after being shown TV ads featuring exceptionally slim and beautiful people.

The same applies to reading fashion magazines. Recent experiments have shown that exposure to magazine photographs of super-thin models produces depression, stress, guilt, shame, insecurity, body-dissatisfaction, and increased endorsement of the thin-ideal stereotype. Magazines like *Vogue* and *Elle* are banned in many eating-disorder clinics, because of their known negative effect on patients' body images.

Most teens watch an average of twenty-two hours of TV a week and are deluged with images of fat-free bodies in the pages of health, fashion, and teen magazines. TV, billboards, and magazines mean that we see "beautiful people" all the time, *more often than members of our own family,* making exceptional good looks seem real, normal, and attainable.

I suggest you simply toss out most of today's teen magazines and hold firm about not letting them make their way back into your young daughter's room. The messages and photographs are so damaging to young girls.

In the same vein, I recommend blowing up your boob tube. I know it sounds radical, but nearly seven years ago, our television antennae was struck by lightening—three times—and we

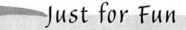

Just for Fun

Great Ways to Encourage Your Daughter to Be Active

Being active means moving more every day. Choose activities that are fun and do them together. Emphasize that being more active makes you both feel better and gives you more energy. It can also help her think and concentrate better, which will help her in school or at work. Activity can help your child feel less bored and depressed, and help you, Mom, handle stress. (Yes, even the stress of raising a preteen daughter!)

- Walk together—to a friend's house, a corner store, around the mall.
- Ride bikes.
- Rollerblade (if you are brave!).
- Take an aerobics class or join a gym.
- Shoot hoops.
- Walk the family dog—or find a neighbor who has a dog and borrow it for a stroll.
- Dance! Take formal classes or just put on a CD and move! I had lots of fun as a little girl making up dances and cheers and backyard "gymnastic" routines with my cousins and friends.
- Go for a nature hike—complete with backpack stuffed with trail mix and water.
- Go for a swim.
- Do an exercise video.
- Wash the car.
- Vacuum the house.
- Do yard work—plant a garden or dig a fish pond.

simply decided not to ask God for another sign. Little did I realize all the benefits that would come from the sudden death of the tube in our living room. For one, Rachel missed all the TV shows and commercials of fashion models parading their bodies and clothes (or lack of them) across the screen on a daily basis. As a result, I am convinced she experienced less angst than the average teenage girl. She was fully thirteen years old before she stopped wearing her hair pulled up in a ponytail and asked to wear lip gloss. In fact, she was much more interested in comfort (loved her jeans and baggy T-shirt) and for those years, much preferred hanging out with her girlfriends than boys. Roll and fix her hair? Makeup? Are you kidding? She didn't have time for the pain. And I didn't press her.

I'll never forget the day Rachel came out of the bathroom for the first day of eighth grade looking like a beauty queen. Her naturally curly hair was styled and flowing down her shoulders, her figure, a slim, lovely hourglass.

My husband's mouth dropped open. "What happened to her?" he asked me as she walked out the door, flipping her curls over her shoulder.

"She blossomed," I answered wistfully, knowing my little girl of yesterday was transforming into a young woman. I was thankful it had happened now, right on schedule, and not too early.

Strongly consider the possibility of limiting or even eliminating the TV in your home during these preteen and teen years. You will never regret it. Or, at the least make a rule that the TV goes off when the weather is pretty outside. An added bonus was that our kids were much more active—going outside to play basketball, riding their bikes—after the television went dark.

Let's Get Real

Need some more ammunition to show our culture's problem with beauty? Read these vital facts and share them with your daughter.

1. Models today weigh 23 percent less than the average woman. Twenty years ago, models weighed only 8 percent less than the average woman.
2. It has been estimated that young women now see more images of outstandingly beautiful women in one day than our mothers saw throughout their entire adolescence.
3. Standards of female beauty have in fact become progressively more unrealistic during the twentieth century. In 1917, the physically perfect woman was about five feet, four inches tall and was well-rounded in figure and form.
4. The current media ideal for women is achievable by less than 5 percent of the female population—and that's just in terms of weight and size. If you want the ideal shape, face etc., it's probably more like 1 percent.
5. Take a look at the ten most popular magazines on the newspaper racks. The women and men on the covers represent about .03 percent of the population. The other 99.97 percent don't have a chance to compete, much less measure up. Don't forget it's a career for these men and women. They're pros. Many have had major body makeovers and have a full-time personal trainer. Most ads are reproduced, airbrushed, or changed by computer. Body parts can be changed at will.
6. Advertising conveys the message "You're not okay. Here's what you need to do to fix what's wrong." Girls and boys believe it and react to it. In a 1997 Body Image Survey, both girls and boys reported that "very thin or muscular models" made them feel insecure about themselves.
7. To measure up to the ideal of the Ken doll, the average man would have to be seven feet, six inches tall, boast a twenty-four-inch neck, a fifty-three-inch chest, and a forty-four-inch waist. And the American Woman? To match the original Barbie doll, she'd tower above the rest of us at eight feet, six inches, flaunt a forty-five-inch bust, and a twenty-six-inch waist.

Boys and Girls — Different Bodies, Different Worries

Let's look at how body image affects boys and girls.

Boys look at their bodies and long for muscle and bulk, especially if they're involved in sports. But a negative body image seems to plague girls more intensely. They look at their bodies and see only the dreaded F word—fat! At ever-younger ages, girls want to be impossibly thin.

All research shows that girls grow to be women who are much more unhappy with their bodies than men. Eight out of ten women criticize their appearance. Hilariously, men actually tend to over-estimate their attractiveness!

Why are women so much more self-critical than men?

Because women are judged on their appearance more than men, and standards of female beauty are considerably higher and more inflexible. Constant exposure to idealized images of female beauty on TV, magazines, and billboards makes exceptional good looks seem normal, and anything short of perfection seem abnormal and ugly.

Boys do go through a short phase of relative dissatisfaction with their appearance in early adolescence, but puberty soon brings them closer to the masculine ideal. For example they get taller, broader in the shoulders, and more muscular. For girls, however, *puberty only makes things worse*. The normal physical changes—an increase in weight and body fat, particularly on the hips and thighs—take them *further* from our culture's obsession with unnatural slimness.

A Harvard University study showed that up to two-thirds of underweight twelve-year-old girls considered themselves to be too fat. (*Did you read that?* This is from *underweight* girls.) By thirteen, at least 50 percent of girls are significantly unhappy about their appearance. By fourteen, focused, specific dissatisfactions have intensified, particularly concerning hips and thighs. By seventeen, only three out of ten girls have not been on a diet—up to eight out of ten will be unhappy with what they see in the mirror.

Forty percent of fifth through eighth grade girls have already dieted. Why? Well, it wasn't to "improve their health." They wanted to look thinner.

Healthy Choices vs. Dieting Treadmill

I am so thankful for our local middle school health teacher—a young woman with a great sense of humor and boundless energy, who emphasized the joy and health of good nutrition. Rather than focusing on diets or what not to eat, she helped a whole class of girls understand and grasp the good things that good food can do for their bodies. In fact, Rachel turned into the "health nut" of the family—loving good food, enjoying exercise, relishing an occasional dessert—but mostly filling her body with fruits, chicken, tuna, and salads because they made her feel better! She even took to making her own healthy lunches to take to school. (Bless her heart, knowing that I'm not fully functional in the mornings, she took this task upon herself. I should also mention that she's one of those naturally organized kids. My *only* naturally organized child.)

I wish I'd had as healthy an attitude about food when I was a teen. When I was in junior high school, I would often skip meals—maybe downing a diet soda for breakfast, eating a quick fast-food lunch, gorging on cookies or sweets when I got home, ruining my appetite for supper, and starting all over again. (Not that my mother didn't try to get me to sit down and eat my oatmeal, mind you. But I was in a hurry!)

The women in our family also had a passionate love for sweets! It was the '70s and dessert was a part of every good Betty Crocker meal. So Mom, my sister, and I would diet, starving ourselves of nutritional food in order to enjoy a really big helping of Saturday's coconut cake or Sunday's Blue Bell

Cookies n' Cream. We all woke up to the damage sugar does to our bodies eventually—but none of us came out unscathed. Once we learned the value of good nutrition, however, we've all been much healthier and happier. (My mother, in her late 60s, shrunk down to a size that any preteen would envy! I,

Rave Reviews

Great Magazines for Girls

Brio is a wonderful, wholesome, uplifting magazine for girls from Focus on the Family. Check it out at www.briomag.org or call 1–800–A–Family and ask about this resource.

Shine magazine is a Christian-based magazine for women filled with articles, fashion, and advice. There is a section in each women's issue just for your daughter called "Young Shine." Available at www.shinemagazine.com or call 1–866–53–SHINE.

American Girl magazine is a terrific alternative to the standard teen magazine fare, filled with party ideas, crafts, girl-to-girl advice. See samples or order at www.americangirl.com or 1–800–845–0005.

Book Picks for Her

True Beauty: The Inside Story by Andrea Stephens (Vine Books, 2000)

Through a variety of Scripture readings, thought-provoking questions, and short quizzes, it reveals the best beauty secrets around. It shows you how to cultivate fruits of the spirit to become truly beautiful—in God's sight *and* in the eyes of the world. Andrea writes the "glamour" column for *Brio* magazine.

The Beauty Book: It's a God Thing! by Nancy Rue (Zonderkidz, 2000)

A wonderful, colorful, easy-to-enjoy book in the popular Young Women of Faith series. (See also *The Body Book* and *The Buddy Book* in this series.)

unfortunately, am not there yet. And may never be there. But I'm coming to terms with my fluffy, curvy God-given body as well. I am determined to focus mostly on being healthy, and accept the results, whatever they may be!)

The best (and simplest) healthy eating advice to give your daughter is this: "When you're hungry, eat. When you're full, stop."

This is the simple advice of registered dietician Barbara Storper, founder of Foodplay Productions, Northampton, Massachusetts, a company that stages performances across the country about healthy eating.

"We don't suggest that parents put kids on diets," she says. "It sets up a cycle where people are craving what they can't eat." Instead, have healthy food around the house, don't get over-involved in how much the children are eating, and make exercise a part of daily life. Rather than collapsing on the sofa after dinner, she says, why not take a family walk?

"Encourage them to get involved in things that make them happy," she says. "They should know that exercise is more about movement that makes you feel good than 'I must get this weight off.'"

Body Talk

Is my daughter too young for a body image discussion?

No, No, and again I say No!

We have talked about the sad fact that many teens, especially girls, dislike their bodies—often feeling fat and unattractive, even when the mirror shows otherwise. Self-criticism and poor body image can be a factor in the development of eating disorders such as anorexia nervosa and bulimia. It can also set up the endless cycle of dieting, followed by weight gain, resulting, eventually, in long-term weight problems.

So when is the right time to talk about body issues? According to Kathleen McCoy, Ph.D., "The best time to help your child develop a positive body image is *well before the teen years."* (Emphasis mine.) Recent studies show that girls in the primary grades—those as young as six, seven, and eight—select "ideal weight" drawings, when shown a selection of body types, significantly thinner than their own body shape, demonstrating that our unrealistic cultural ideals of feminine beauty have a negative impact early on.

I remember meeting a young girl at church when I was about thirteen or fourteen years old. She was skeleton thin, but during Sunday school she asked us to pray "that her parents would stop trying to make her eat." I heard that she'd once been chubby but had lost lots of weight over the summer. Too much weight, but she didn't seem to realize it. She asked me over to her home one night and fixed me a huge ice cream sundae, then refused to eat a single bite. I was young, but I knew something was wrong. Sadly, I just didn't know what it was. Neither did her parents. Little was known about anorexia at that time. Tragically, the young girl never made it to adulthood.

Moms, listen closely: Studies show that when parents— especially mothers—criticize their daughter's weight and appearance, these girls are more likely to develop eating disorders in adolescence. Certainly this is not always the case; more is being discovered about anorexia every day and there are other possible causes. Some scientists think that there may be a seratonin-related connection. We don't want to burden hurting parents with this finding, but it pays to be conscious that parents' obsessions with physical perfection can be detrimental to their kids.

Your Role

What can you do to help your daughter feel good about herself physically?

Point out the fact that healthy, attractive people come in all sizes and shapes. A wonderful book for larger-sized, larger-boned girls to read is *True Beauty* by the beautiful, plus-sized model Emme. It has some great pictures of pretty, normal-sized, Emme, as a big-boned adolescent. In it, Emme says, "We are all built differently, and yet every woman I know has at one time or another tried to fit herself into some perverse notion of what she should look like. What a waste!" She goes on to add, "If the image makers and pharmaceutical companies and fashion designers have their way, we will always be made to feel that we don't fit. Either we don't fit the clothes, or we don't fit the ideal, or we don't fit the lifestyle. We just don't fit, period. We're being sold an image of superthin, superfit supermodel, but that's not who we are, not by a couple of sizes."

Here are several things you can do to help foster a positive body image in your young teen:

- Focus on what's really important—teens' values, character, and behavior—much more than their looks.
- Don't communicate your own weight concerns to your teen. Parents who put a high value on physical attractiveness and being thin communicate this to their teens and place them at risk for being weight conscious.
- Let girls know that weight gain during puberty is not only natural, but essential for healthy development. She's a work in progress! Your daughter may put on weight before her body has fully grown, and may look a bit chunky for a while. She needs to know this is normal and that she isn't any less attractive or fun to be with because of it.
- Keep your comments positive and realistic. A girl in early puberty (which can occur, in some, as early as nine or ten) may experience a significant weight gain

as the normal body shape changes from angular to rounded. This is a normal passage of adolescence and should not be viewed with alarm and criticism by parents. It can help to reassure your daughter that her new shape is a positive sign of many more changes to come as she grows from little girl to woman.

- If your daughter is very overweight, emphasize good health and fitness as a family instead of singling out the overweight child for a special regimen. Family health and togetherness—rather than attractiveness —can be a much more positive goal.

- We need to touch and hug our daughters as we verbally approve of their inner and outer beauty: People suffering from extreme body-image disturbance report a lack of holding and hugging as children.

- Have no tolerance for teasing—especially about unchangeable physical appearances—in your family. If your child is being teased mercilessly at school for her appearance, do everything you can to have it stopped immediately, going through whatever channels necessary, even moving to another school if need be. Studies show that children who are teased about flaws in their appearance (particularly size or weight) as a child or teen often have their body image permanently disturbed.

- Remember even our very pretty girls are often insecure. There *are* disadvantages to being attractive: attractive people are under much greater pressure to maintain their appearance. (Think of the disproportionate number of unhappy "beautiful people" in glamorous Hollywood marriages.) Also, studies show that attractive people often don't trust praise of their work or talents, believing positive evaluations to be influenced by their appearance. Pretty

women and young girls often don't know if others
love them for their inner qualities or simply admire
and fawn over them because they happen to be
beautiful.

Mirror, Mirror, What's the Balance?

Now comes the balance. Our daughters must live in this
world with others, and their life will be easier if they do all they
can with what they've been given physically—as long as it is
not in excess, resulting in an obsession with perfection. Consider these sad, but true facts:

- Attractive children are more popular, both with class-
  mates and teachers. Teachers give higher evaluations
  to the work of attractive children and have higher
  expectations of them (which has been shown to
  improve performance).
- Attractive applicants have a better chance of getting
  jobs, and of receiving higher salaries. (One U.S. study
  found that taller men earned around $600 per inch
  more than shorter executives.)
- In court, attractive people are found guilty less often.
  When found guilty, they receive less severe sentences.
- The "bias for beauty" operates in almost all social
  situations—all experiments show we react more
  favorably to physically attractive people.

Though the Bible warns of beauty being a snare, beauty is
evident everywhere in God's glorious creation, and we all are
drawn to beautiful things. We feel better about ourselves when
we look our best. My mother used to repeat the adage, "A thing
of beauty is a joy forever." We are free to enjoy beauty—the
beauty of creation, including our own bodies—as soon as we
conquer any obsessions with absolute perfection.

One day I was thinking and walking and it was as if the Lord spoke to my heart saying, "Becky, you are only free to appreciate what you stop demanding." This poignant truth relates to so many areas—relationships, jobs, and, yes, our body images. As soon as we stop demanding that we meet up to some air-brushed image of physical perfection (and pass that healthy attitude to our daughters), we are free to help them appreciate all the beautiful things about their faces and bodies and thoroughly enjoy the female bent to "decorate" ourselves.

With a healthy view of body image intact, we are free to move on to the pure wholesome fun of "decorating" ourselves, something us women—with a God-given affinity for beautiful things—have enjoyed through the ages.

God, Mom, and Me

In the movie *Little Women,* there is a scene where Marmie is combing her daughter's lovely hair and says what I believe to be one of the most profound statements a mother can make to her daughter: "I only care what you think of yourself. If you feel your value lies in being merely decorative, I fear that someday you might find yourself believing that's all you really are. Time erodes all such beauty. But what it cannot diminish is the wonderful workings of your mind—your humor, your kindness, and your moral courage. These are the things I cherish so in you."

Write this quote out for your daughter on a pretty piece of paper in calligraphy or a nice font from your computer and suggest she keep it somewhere where she can read it now and then. Tell her, "You are lovely and, truly, your beauty is a pleasure to behold. But I want you to read this line from Marmie and know that what I most cherish in you is the beauty you carry inside your heart. And these are the things God cherishes most in you as well."

Then, together, look up and read 1 Peter 3:3–4. *The Living Bible*'s translation is great: "Don't be concerned about the outward beauty that depends on jewelry, or beautiful clothes, or hair arrangement. Be beautiful inside, in your hearts, with the lasting charm of a gentle and quiet spirit which is so precious to God."

Give your daughter another pretty piece of paper and let her type or write out this verse to keep as a reminder of her truest, innermost beauty.

chapter three

Lip Gloss, Hair Gel, and Toe Rings

Having Fun with Outer Beauty

Maureen is my "wuhnduhful" friend from Georgia, a beautician by trade and the fascinating subject of a chapter in my book *Real Magnolias*, about southern women who have influenced my life. Though, like the exuberant hairdresser from *Steel Magnolias*, she prefers to be called a "glamour technician."

I will never forget the first time I met Maureen. I was in the backseat of a friend's car waiting for her to come out the front door of her little blue and white cottage.

When she appeared, Maureen didn't just walk down the steps, she *sashayed* down them on clouds of giggles. Her hair was a perfectly coiffed ball of blond fluff. Scarlet lipstick outlined a smile as welcoming as a Southern morning. Her bountiful figure epitomized the word *voluptuous*. She smelled of honeysuckle and apple blossoms and exuded womanly sensuality, in the best sense of the word. Not raw sexuality, but the air of a secure woman who was aware of, and grateful for, every inch of her femininity. If there had been a theme song to accompany Maureen's stroll down the sidewalk runway, I'm sure it would have been "I Enjoy Being a Girl."

The first words out of Maureen's bright red lips completed the charming picture, blending her inner beauty with her outer glow. She extended her well-manicured hand and said, "What a blessin' it is to finally meet you! I've been looking fohward to this all week, and I just know we're goin' to be good friends."

And she was right. Before the week's end at a girlfriend's getaway at Calloway Gardens, Maureen, four other ladies, and I had not only bonded emotionally and spiritually—we had all been given makeovers! By the time Maureen had teased, combed, sprayed, and painted us, we could have given Dolly Parton and the Magnolias a run for their money. It was such fun.

Chick Chat

Ask your daughter what features she likes most about her face and body.

Then tell her some of the things you think are especially pretty and unique to the way God made her, inside and out.

Big Hair Day

When I was a girl of ten or twelve, my creative cousin loved to tease our hair and create a big hairdo for all of us kids. (We live near Dallas, where big hair was born.) The only materials needed were a comb, a can of hairspray, and a mirror to admire ourselves in. Oh, and big bottles of shampoo and conditioner to wash out the oversized hairdos— before going back to school or being seen in public.

On a summer afternoon when your daughter whines she is bored, get out the comb and Aqua Net and let her go at it, promising to take pictures when she has completed her masterpiece.

I had to remind myself that Maureen is outside of the standard "model" of what is considered magazine-beautiful in today's media. Yet she carries herself with such self-assurance, is so positive and focused on others, and uses her artistic talent in makeup, dress, and hairstyle, that she is a compellingly attractive woman. God works through Maureen every day as she shines her pretty, loving light into the little beauty shop behind her blue cottage. While she washes and combs and styles, she also listens and soothes and gives advice (I call it "beauty shop therapy"). By the time she lets her customers talk out their problems and transforms their lifeless hair into works of art, Maureen has probably lifted more spirits of women in her small town than the local pastor! Helping others become beautiful on the outside has become a way for her to show God's love from the inside.

It is a wonderful, balanced way to view the gift of beauty—for there is nothing wrong in wanting to make ourselves look as pretty as possible, especially for special occasions.

Here are some great ideas to inspire you and your daughter to enjoy the art of decorating yourselves for fun and pleasure!

Dressing Modestly

I heard wise and witty Jill Briscoe, with her charming British accent, today on the radio. She was sharing the tragic Old Testament story of David's sin with Bathsheba. She was curious as to why Bathsheba might have been exposing herself in such an open way—bathing on the roof. Jill concluded the story with a warning of modesty for young women: "If you want to be a Bathsheba, there's always a David waiting nearby." David should not have taken Bathsheba—another man's wife—into his bed. And of course, David was held responsible for his sin and suffered tragic consequences in the loss of the child conceived from their union. But perhaps Bathsheba might have caused David to avoid temptation had she been more careful about when and where she took a bath. Most often, when sexual sin occurs, it takes two to complete the tango. When girls dress provocatively, most red-blooded guys will respond with lustful thoughts—even if they truly don't want to be tempted. A wise mother is frank about life in the real world, and will warn her daughter that she can cause boys—and men (scary thought!)—to stumble into sinful thoughts by the way she dresses.

You can help your daughter learn modesty by doing the following:

1. Encourage her to become a bit of a spy. Help her observe women who are attractively, but modestly, dressed. Discuss the definition of modesty and what is and isn't appropriate. (This will need to be a family decision, even though she might balk at it.)

2. Choose your battles carefully. For example, you might let holes in the knees of the jeans pass even though you don't like the style—but fight for shirts that cover her midsection.

3. Have your husband or an older brother talk about the issues of respect as it relates to how a young girl or woman dresses and explain why there are just some things that young girls shouldn't wear. My mother had some success using the word "mystery" with me—I can hear her speech on bikinis even now: "Becky, give the boys something to wonder about. Create a mystery—no need to bare it all. There's nothing *interesting* about that!"

What about piercings, tattoos, and dying their hair?

We had a rule that our children could not do anything to themselves that couldn't grow back or be undone. Scott also insisted that the only people in our family who could wear pierced earrings also had to wear a bra. That pretty much limited the ear piercings to the females in our family. At least until they were eighteen. I have to admit, our oldest son—our challenge child—went out and got pierced, tattooed, and dyed—all on his eighteenth birthday. After I recovered from the shock, I found I still loved him. Thankfully, the trend didn't last long and all but the tattoo of a large tree on his back, which is with us for a lifetime, are but a shadow of a memory. I guess the tree will grow old, shrivel, and wrinkle as he does (the mighty oak looking more like a weeping willow). At least he won't be alone, since most of his generation will be sporting small, shriveled tattoos on odd places as they lie in a nursing home together some day.

Another good solution is to let kids try some of the latest crazy fads during the summer break. Gabe, our youngest son of raven black hair, had his hair bleached blond one summer while we were in Florida, followed by a lovely—but brief—stint where he sported a bright blue "do." It was summertime, so there was no school, and we didn't know anyone in Florida. It was a great time to let him experiment with very little angst on our part. Rachel also experimented with some highlighting and more subdued home coloring kits—all during the summer months. By the time school started, she had been through a few bad hair

Just for Fun

Mom and Me Glamour Photos

When Rachel turned thirteen I took her to the mall and we had our "glamour photos" done—both wearing a pretty straw hat with fat pink roses on it. The price of the photos included getting our hair and makeup done, along with a variety of "costumes" to put on. You could do the same thing at home with some creativity and a good friend with a camera!

days and had figured out what worked for her, and in spite of my concerns, I have to admit, she looked great!

Coloring doesn't usually hurt your daughter's hair texture if you want to help her experiment with a home coloring kit. But any type of bleaching, highlighting, or frosting can give them a fried look they probably want to avoid. Better save this for a professional.

Rachel's hair is curly and can be frizzy. We found the best way to get help for taming her mane was to ask another girl with pretty, similar hair what products she used. Don't be shy about asking someone where she got her hair cut or what mousse she uses—most girls love to share the information and will appreciate the compliment.

And what of toe rings? Since the title promised I'd touch on this, I have to tell you I think they are really cute. I even bought one so I could feel hip and with it when I was barefoot at the beach—until I caught it on a seashell and for the rest of the week I had a really hip-and-with-it toe cut. I just can't seem to get the hang of being cool.

Never Too Old to Play Dress-Up

No matter how old your daughter is, she will never be too old to play dress-up. Here are some ideas to get you dressed up for fun.

My cousin Jamie would search for prom dresses and brides-maid gowns at bargain prices at Goodwill or garage sales. Then she would take up enormous seams in the sides and bodices, cut off the excess material, and make delightfully glamorous play clothes for her daughters. They felt like fairy princesses, and Jamie's "dress-up box" was quite the popular neighborhood play place for little girls.

As your daughter matures, you can still have a blast playing "dress-up" by taking her clothes shopping, along with one of her good friends. In addition to buying sensible school clothes, let the girls try on fancy ball gowns and prom dresses. Bring your camera and capture the Pretty Girl moments as they admire themselves in Cinderella attire in the department store mirror.

Musical moms: Learn the words to the song "I Feel Pretty," and have fun singing a couple of refrains to your daughter as she looks in the mirror when she's really gone all out to look her best. You can hear the song, in all its charm and lightness, on the video or soundtrack of *West Side Story*. Warning: Only try this at home. No belting out show tunes in the department store. Not that I haven't tried it a time or two with my own children, but the results weren't pretty. Someday I'm planning to put together a little album of my own: *Ditties To Embarrass Your Children By*.

For a fun activity with lots of girls (Girl Scouts, Sunday school party, Awana's fun night), partner with several other moms and pull together resources—old prom dresses, costume jewelry, sequined shoes, gloves, etc. Let your most organized moms create a well-organized "dressing room" for your little stars. Have several portable lighted mirrors or vanities set up for doing hair and makeup. Have your performance-oriented moms take turns with a karaoke set and ham it up as your models tour the runway. Let the girls make up their own "bios." For example, "Misty is from sunny California." Have "Misty" emerge with huge sunglasses. "She loves to catch waves and rays." If dads and siblings are willing to be an audience, even better. Make a fun family night out of it and let the "models" serve cookies and tea on silver platters to the "guests" after the show.

Runway Dreams

Brie, a fourteen-year-old girl, admitted, "I know it's silly and superficial to want to look like a model, but it would make life so much easier."[2]

---

[2] Quoted in *How to Mother a Successful Daughter* (Three Rivers Press, 1998).

Does your daughter dream of being a fashion model? What girl (or woman!) hasn't felt like Brie on occasion?

Check out www.modelsforchrist.com together. The founder of this support organization for Christian fashion models said, "It's not easy mixing modeling and morality. But a handful of top New York models have managed to hold on to their values—and their careers." The website contains some wonderful testimonies about the reality of the emptiness of beauty and fame without Christ, and the power of using God's gifts of physical beauty in a fashion or modeling career. The website may help temper the illusion that looking like a model is utopia. Or check out www.tonyasquest.com to learn about former model Tonya Ruiz's story.

Rave Reviews

Some worth-the-investment resources are from Klutz Books (www.klutz.com). It is hard to beat the value and simplicity of a Klutz book for learning how to do so many things kids love. And you've got to love a publishing-toy company started by three guys who peddled their first three thousand books by backpack and bicycle.

Hair Book. Wonder how they do those wonderful complicated-looking braids and hairstyles? This is a perfect book for preteen and teen girls with lots of full-color pictures and easy-to-follow directions.

Braids and Bows. This book is similar to the *Hair Book,* but for younger girls, ages four to thirteen, with moms' assistance. Includes complete directions for making your own barrettes and hair ornaments with the goodies provided.

Hair Wraps. This book includes embroidery thread and ribbon to achieve those fun, colorful Jamaican styles!

Nail Art. Shows tips, techniques, and hundreds of designs to paint on fingernails and toenails. The nail paints are nontoxic and peel off—so girls as young as six can join in the fun.

The Body Book. This is an instructional book of simple recipes for things like bath salts, tub infusions, hair rinses, facial masks, toners, and scrubs. Comes complete with a spa box of supplies that includes a facial brush, nail buffer, pumice stone, bath infusion bag, headband, three vials of essential oils (lavender, peppermint, and tangerine), and more.

Kitchen Table Makeovers

What preteen girl—or mom—doesn't enjoy getting a full-blown makeover? For the easy route, call a professional to come into your home. You can find a Mary Kay consultant in your area by going to www.marykay.com or by checking your local newspaper or yellow page listings. This company—started by an amazing Christian woman—has recently developed a whole new line of cosmetics for young teens called "Velocity." In fact, some very "hip" eighteen- to twenty-year-old girls are showing and selling the product line. It is a plus for young girls if the makeup consultant is closer to their age. At no cost to you, you can host a "teen party" and a beauty consultant will treat your daughter and her friends to a skin care and makeup party. She will show them how to have a natural pretty glow that doesn't look cheap or made-up.

If you do this for a small birthday party, you might consider giving each girl $5.00–$10.00 (depending on your budget and how many girls come) to spend on lip gloss or eye shadow as a party favor. Make sure you tell the consultant ahead of time not to pressure the girls into buying a product at the party. They can take a catalog home and, if they—or their moms—want to purchase products later, that can be done. However, you will probably want to purchase a few beauty products of your own to make the visit worth the consultant's time. The information from Mary Kay is wonderful, and the makeup is great, but it can be too expensive for preteen and teenage budgets. Still, the girls can apply what they learn with other products they can afford.

Don't forget to take before and after pictures of all the girls!

Throw a Beauty Party!

Even girls who are too young to wear makeup enjoy playing with beauty. My friend Jane Jarrell gave her young daughter a Beauty Party for her birthday and it was a huge hit. Here are her great ideas:

Make Hand Cookies

Trace a child's hand on a piece of construction paper. Purchase some sugar cookie dough and sprinkle your counter top with powdered sugar. Roll the tube of dough out to about 1/4 inch. Put the construction paper hand on the dough and cut around the shape with a knife. Or buy a hand-shaped cookie cutter.

Make several colors of icing—with powdered sugar, a little milk, and food coloring. Paint the cookie "nails."

Put out lots of little bowls of Skittles, M&M's, sprinkles, jimmies—anything with color. Use these candies for rings and bracelets or nail designs—using the icing as "glue."

Spray Paint Hair

Use washable hair spray paint. Jane used pink and red to match all the balloons in the house.

Video and Manicure

Buy a variety of nail colors and let the little girls choose a favorite shade. Then you can paint their nails one at a time while *Mary-Kate and Ashley's Fashion Party* video is playing. For older girls, let them paint each other's nails while watching *The Princess Diaries* or *My Fair Lady*.

Fashion Show Fun

Provide a dress-up box and let the girls put on a fashion show with you hamming it up as the announcer as they walk on to the living room "stage." "Here we have Katie, who is wearing that 'I am Spring' look, with a fashionable plastic daisy poking out of her fuchsia straw hat." You get the idea. A French accent, if you can fake one, will add to the fun. If the girls are older, you may have a natural ham in the group who could take over the announcing duties.

Party Favor Ideas

1. Decorate the perimeter of wooden picture frames with Barbie shoes, cheap hair accessories, and plastic nail polish bottles.
2. Take each girl's picture with them showing their nails and hair style.
3. Fill makeup bags with nail polish, glitter lip color, and lotion.

You can join in the fun and spray paint your hair as you take on the role of an outrageous manicurist-pedicurist as Jane did.

Beauty Cake

Buy any premade cake from the bakery and tuck in small, new beauty items, and a few ribbons and bows for a "Beauty Parlor Cake" look.

Other great party ideas can be found on Jane's website, www.janejarrell.net.

Spa — At Home

For more mother-daughter beauty fun, tell your daughter that you are going to have a "spa morning" or "spa evening" together. Take turns taking a nice hot bubble bath. (If your hot water heater is anything like ours, you may have to allow thirty minutes between your long, hot bubble baths if both of you want a hot bath!) Then get wrapped up in fluffy robes and house slippers or socks. (A quick comfort trick: toss the towels, robes, and socks in a dryer for a few minutes and they will be toasty warm when she exits the tub. I've even resorted to blow drying my socks for a second to warm my cold tootsies.) Light some scented candles, put on some soft music. Or put on a wonderful old Rogers and Hammerstein musical like *South Pacific, The King and I,* or *The Sound of Music.* Or an even older Bing Crosby movie like *Going My Way* or *White Christmas* if you are in an upbeat toe-tapping mood. This gives you both background music for you to sing along with, and a story line to follow as well.

Set out nice lotions, polish remover, nail files, pumice stones, and pretty nail polish. You might even let her choose a special lotion from Bath and Body Works. They often have great clearance sales and small sample items that are easy on the budget.

Take turns painting each other's toenails and fingernails, putting cotton balls between your toes for the authentic look. If your daughter is not old enough to paint your fingernails for you, let her try your toenails. No one will see them if you do this in the wintertime when you wear close-toed shoes, and she will feel important.

Slather on lots of lotion, then cuddle up with a couple of quilts and finish watching the movie, feeling beautiful inside and out.

This could also be fun for a slumber party or for a Females in the Family Only Night, or maybe you could ask another mother-daughter pair to join you for Chick Flick Spa Night!

What's Cooking, Beautiful?

For a beauty party or spa night, you might like to try these fun recipes for bubble bath, lip gloss, and other beauty products to make in your own kitchen.

Basic Bubble Bath

Ingredients:
5 drops fragrant oil or essential oil
1 quart water
1 bar castile soap (grated or flaked)
1 1/2 ounces glycerin

Directions:
Mix all ingredients together. Store in a container. Pour in running water.

Lip Gloss

Ingredients:
Paraffin wax
Coconut oil
Petroleum jelly
Candy melts (to color the gloss and make it taste sweet)
Oil-based candy flavoring (if you want a special flavor)
Grater
Wax paper
Ziploc bag
Small container (recycle old makeup containers or 35mm film containers, or look in stores that carry beads, crafts, or fishing tackle)

Directions:
Grate some paraffin wax onto wax paper. Measure 1/4 teaspoon grated wax into the plastic bag. Add 1 teaspoon coconut oil, 1 teaspoon petroleum jelly, and 1

candy melt. Add 1/8 teaspoon oil-based candy flavoring if you like.

Seal the bag and carefully put it in a bowl of hot tap water to melt ingredients, about three to five minutes. (Use tap water! Never use a microwave or stove to heat the water.)

Once all the ingredients are melted, remove the bag from the water. Working quickly, squish ingredients around in bag to mix. Clip off a tiny corner of the bag and squeeze gloss into the clean container. Let it set for an hour, or put it in the refrigerator for fifteen minutes.

Use a cotton swab instead of your finger to apply gloss. Your lip gloss should last a long time. If it changes color, odor, or texture, though, throw it away.

Fruity-Tooty Facials for All Three Skin Types

Just Peachy Facial (Normal Skin)
Ingredients:
1 medium peach
1 tablespoon honey
oatmeal

Directions:
Cook peach until it is soft, mash with a fork, add honey and oatmeal until it is a thick consistency. Apply to skin. Let sit for ten minutes, then rinse well with cool water.

Banana Bash Facial (Dry Skin)
Ingredients:
2 medium bananas
Honey (optional)

Directions:
Mash bananas with a fork. Don't overmash or it will be too runny. Add honey if desired. Smooth over skin, let sit for ten minutes, and rinse off with cool water.

Sweet Strawberry Facial (Oily Skin)
Ingredients:
8–9 whole strawberries
3 tablespoons honey

Directions:
Using a fork, mash strawberries into a pulp, then add honey. Mix. Don't overblend or it will be runny. Apply directly to the skin, let sit for a few minutes, then rinse off.

Do *not* use any of these recipes if you know you are allergic to any of the fruit. Some people have allergic reactions to strawberries; your daughter probably already knows if she's one of them!

These recipes can be found at www.pioneerthinking.com, a fun website for all sorts of homemade products.

God, Mom, and Me

Read the story of Queen Esther together from a modern paraphrase—a chapter a night or so over a week. It reads like a novel, so your daughter won't be bored. Then ask and talk through the following questions:

1. If God makes some people physically beautiful, how does he expect them to use this gift? How did Esther use and enhance her gift of beauty? What physical gifts has God given you that you can use to bring honor to him?
2. Does God love pretty people more than ugly people? God made many beautiful things and many beautiful people—but what about a girl or a woman does God value the most? (See Proverbs 31:30: "Charm is deceptive, and beauty is fleeting; but a woman who fears the Lord is to be praised.")
3. Is it okay to be beautiful? To make ourselves look prettier?

Now that we are all relaxed and beautified, we're ready to enter the roller coaster journey through the three Ps: Periods, PMS, and Puberty. It will be a bumpy ride, but don't worry, moms, I'll hand out some coping seatbelts in the next chapter.

She's an Emotional Girl

Dealing with the Three Ps: Periods, PMS, and Puberty

When my youngest son, Gabe, was in first grade, he came home from school, plopped his backpack on the kitchen table, sat down, sighed, and put his head in his hands.

"Bad day?" I asked.

"Terrible," he answered. Then, with arms outstretched for emphasis, he added, "There's this new boy in my class, and all he does is whine and gripe all day! He has the worst case of PMS I've ever seen in a kid!"

Poor Gabe. All he knew about PMS was that it signaled bad moods. I had never paused to explain what it was or that it only affected postpubescent girls. (My friend, fellow writer, and PMS-sufferer Rebecca Barlow Jordan refers to PMS as Pre-Monster Syndrome.)

My episodes of PMS—especially in my late twenties and thirties—are legendary. There was the awful time one of the kids stepped on my last nerve as I was hauling in the groceries. Upon some small provocation, I turned and hurled an entire gallon of milk at the wall in the hallway whereupon it burst and dramatically spilled its contents—something I regretted for weeks thereafter as the odor of sour milk in the carpet wafted through the house. The next month I overheard one of my sons say to the other one: "Better not make Mom mad right now. She's standing near dairy products."

Hormones fall on all womankind, though admittedly with variance in fury. When your daughter begins to enter the Puberty Zone, there will be two of you dealing with roller coaster emotions. If she has sisters, your husband and any brothers in the family should probably purchase a cabin in the woods where they can periodically escape for their own sanity and safety.

Gabe, now fifteen, casually made an observation the other day that I thought was so profound I paused to write it down. He said, "Mom, you know what? If men acted like women act, they would be considered completely insane."

Although the statement, at face value, sounds pretty prejudiced, I have to laugh at the truth around its edges. If a girlfriend shows up at my door and she's crying and says, "I need a hug. Can I come in and have a nervous breakdown at your kitchen table?" I would think nothing of it. I'd immediately give her the hug and a cup of tea and any morsels of chocolate or cheesecake I could scrounge up. But if a man did the same thing, I would be tempted to call 9-1-1.

And yet, there's something wonderful, mysterious, and exciting about being female with such a wide array of feelings and emotions. God made no mistakes when he created us women with such tender hearts and feelings so near the surface. It is these precious hearts and emotions that also cause women to be the great comforters and nurturers in our homes and in the world.

Knowing how difficult it is to balance our own womanly emotions and hormonal cycles, we are uniquely able to help guide and assure our own daughters as they roller coaster through the journey from young girl to teen to woman.

I've pulled together the best ideas I can find to help you help her. (And possibly help yourself along the way!)

The Big P: Periods — Yes, You Have to Have One

Of course, no chapter on rising and falling moods would be complete without talking about where they come from—namely, our hormones. These hormones are in full bloom as your daughter nears twelve and thirteen. The first and most noticeable rite of passage, her first period, brings a whole new set of emotions with it.

We'll get to those, but first a Period Primer to help you prepare your daughter for the many delights of menstruation.

Common Questions Girls Have about Menstruating

When will I start?

Most girls begin having a period between the ages of ten and sixteen.

How often does it happen?

Near the end of the teen years, her cycles will come about every twenty-eight days. But until then, most girls have very irregular periods.

Does it hurt?

Most girls only experience a slight cramping and small amount of discomfort in their abdomen or lower back.

How much blood will I lose?

The amount of blood lost can range from one to eight tablespoons.

Girls should be told that the blood is released very slowly over two to eight days and may range in color from light brown to bright red to very dark maroon.

How will it happen, and what will I do?

Usually, she will see blood on her underwear, a bit in the toilet, or on toilet paper. If she starts her period and doesn't have a pad, she can ask for one from the nurse or teacher if she is at school. Or if she's away from home, she can borrow one from a friend or a friend's mother or older sister. In a pinch, several layers of toilet paper will do until she can get a pad.

As my friend Annette Smith put it in her helpful, well-written book, *Help! My Little Girl's Growing Up!*: "Be truthful about menstruation. Periods aren't particularly pleasant, but neither are they awful. They are, in fact, an *outside* sign that everything *inside* is working as it should."

Celebrating the Big Day in a Special Way

Most daughters feel a little uneasy and embarrassed about their dad commenting on their starting their period. She knows you will tell him and that is enough. Dads are probably safest just commenting casually on what a wonderful little girl he has, and how proud he is of the way she is growing up into a young woman.

My husband, Scott, found a necklace with a locket style heart in two separate pieces that he gave to Rachel on her twelfth birthday, soon after she had her first period. He told her she was to keep half of the heart, and when she found the man she wanted to marry, he was to present Scott with her half of the heart. Scott would know this is the man she wanted to be with for the rest of her life. Scott would then give the young man the other piece of the heart on their wedding day to symbolize two becoming one.

Last week, a very nervous young man entered the living room and asked to speak to my husband. In one hand he held an engagement ring he wanted to give to our daughter, in the other hand he held the other half of the heart locket. It was a beautiful way for our daughter to honor the two men that she loved. I would suggest that any father wanting to celebrate his daughter's entrance into womanhood do something like this— perhaps a week or so after she starts her period—to acknowledge something special has occurred without embarrassing her.

Moms too can think of a special way to celebrate this rite of passage that communicates, "You are on your way to becoming a woman, and I recognize and applaud that!" Perhaps the day she starts her period is the day you give her permission to get her ears pierced or buy her first pair of high-heeled shoes or wear pantyhose or get a set of acrylic nails.

You might even rent a convertible with the top down, and surprise (shock?) her by picking her up from school, your hair blowing in the breeze, and say, "Hey Babe, we're goin' out on the town, just us women." Then take her to a chick flick or a special restaurant, just the two of you. It will be a token of fun times to come, when the two of you will become not only mother and daughter, but also very good friends who will have lots of fun together.

Using Humor to Lighten Menstrual Moments

One of the best ways I've found to deal with potentially embarrassing topics around periods and sanitary products is to use liberal doses of humor. Used correctly, humor can promote a lot of female bonding in the family!

For example, we use girls-only nicknames for female things: My mother and I had a code word for menstrual supplies like pads and tampons: Rosebuds. I handed the code word down to my daughter. Typically she uses it in conversations like, "Mom, when you go to the store, be sure to pick up some shampoo, milk, and don't forget a bouquet of *rosebuds*." (Wink, wink.)

When Rachel was old enough to want to try to use tampons, I allowed her to do this, knowing how much easier it would be for her to handle her period without dealing with bulky pads. (As I recall she was around thirteen or fourteen.) One afternoon, when all of the boys were gone, I gave her a box of small tampons along with the printed instruction sheet. I proceeded to tell her a few hints on insertion, both of us trying to keep a straight face, and then told her if she had any problems to holler at me and I'd come to the door to coach her. Within a few minutes I heard her yell, "MOM! I think this thing is too big for me! It won't go in!"

Without missing a beat I calmly yelled back, "Hold on just a second. I'll run and get you the hammer."

"That is NOT funny!" she retorted. But I could hear her laughing even from outside the door.

Tonight, as I was typing this very chapter, a couple from the neighborhood dropped by for coffee. The woman asked for a packet of Sweet 'N Low and I handed her a little bowl of the pink packets I try to keep handy on the kitchen counter.

"Oh," she laughed. "This is interesting . . ."

To my horror she was holding a small, pink, unopened, plastic-wrapped mini-pad in her hands, plucked from the bowl of sweeteners.

While I was cleaning the house in a hurry, I must have picked up the pink-covered pad somewhere in the bathroom and—having taken temporary leave of my senses—seeing only that it was pink and small, I mistook it for a Sweet 'N Low packet and tucked it in the bowl.

"My friends always ask me if you really do these crazy and embarrassing things in your books," came the comment I've heard dozens of times over the years. "I always tell them, 'Yes, and even more things than you can imagine.'"

Just for Fun

Share these with your daughter for a little comic relief.

Bumper Stickers by PMSing Women:

- God Made Us Sisters; Prozac Made Us Friends.
- Don't Treat Me Any Differently Than You Would Treat the Queen.
- If You Want Breakfast in Bed, Sleep in the Kitchen.
- I'm Out of Estrogen—and I Have a Gun.
- Guys Have Feelings Too, But Like ... Who Cares?
- Next Mood Swing: 6 Minutes.
- All Stressed Out and No One to Choke.
- I'm One of Those Bad Things That Happen to Good People.
- You—Off My Planet!

Moody Blues and Bright Skies

If there is one book I recommend every mom, daughter, and husband read (besides this one of course!) it is *Emotional Phases of a Woman's Life* by Jean Lush. In her book Jean describes how a woman's feelings rise and fall with estrogen and progesterone levels in her body.

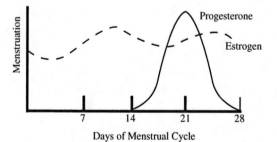

Days of Menstrual Cycle

Keep in mind that these examples are true for girls and women with strong mood fluctuations. Many females hardly notice a difference from week to week. I once read that PMS generally gets worse for a woman after she has given birth to multiple children. I believe it. But I don't know if it is because of hormone changes or because coping with three or four preschoolers would send anyone to the stark edge of sanity.

Read the following and share with your daughter—if either one of you rides hormonal tidal waves. It helps so much to know why we feel blue and sad some days, and why we feel we want to hug the whole world the following week. If the men in your family are being affected by your hormone cycle, share this with them as well. My husband has learned to be extra sweet to me during PMS—to bring me hot tea and a quilt and encourage me to cocoon for a nap. Then, of course, he locks and bolts the door for three days.

The First Week (After Menstruation)
- Estrogen levels rising
- Self-directed, disciplined
- Outgoing
- Task oriented and focused
- Reasonable
- Optimistic

Second Week
- Estrogen levels off and declines slightly
- Blue skies—good, warm, summer-like feelings; happy, hopeful, and easygoing
- Sense of well-being, inner strength
- Less assertive, more realistic goals than first week
- Peaceful
- Not bothered by small irritations
- Idealistic dreams and goals for self and family
- Sensitive to the loveliness of environment
- Creative, with positive energy
- Feels reasonable and tolerant of self and others

Ovulation

- Estrogen rising again, progesterone rising (24-hour period sometime during the end of the second week. Usually ten days following the end of period.)
- Passive, introverted
- Passive, receptive (patient, accepting, open-minded)
- Content
- Nurturing feelings
- Especially attracted to opposite sex (Note to Mothers: This is when you have to lock your daughter in her room. Just kidding, but you know how *you* feel around this time of the month. My husband would like to nominate Ovulation as a national holiday.)
- Enjoys various roles

I have found that on the day of ovulation I have cravings that I had during pregnancy: anything salty and sour, like pickles or Italian dressing on salads (or by the spoonful!).

Third Week

- Rising estrogen and overriding progesterone
- Subject to variable feelings: some good and some bad days—up and down feelings
- Moody and gloomy—a sense of feeling doomed
- Apprehensive for no apparent reason
- Feeling immobilized
- Doubting herself
- Slowing down—disliking pressure
- Discouraged
- Less friendly and outgoing
- Losing sense of well-being
- Longing for more peaceful life
- Impatient with others
- Losing interest in goals and plans, bored

- Lacking coordination and clarity of thought (My sister and I have dubbed this fogginess "PMS Head.")

Fourth Week: Premenstrual—Estrogen and Progesterone Levels Fall
- Very reactive, irritable, touchy, nervous
- Moody, unstable
- Unable to concentrate
- Sensitive to noise
- Unpredictable outbursts of emotions
- Quarrelsome
- Childlike, unreasonable
- Lack of self-confidence
- Loss of interest in hobbies and tasks
- Melancholy, withdrawn
- Awkward, shaky
- Food binges, craves sweets—especially chocolate or spices

Chick Chat

When She Cries

When your daughter gets weepy, don't try to tease her out of it. Just soothe her and assure her that you understand how she feels. If you suspect her upset is hormone related, and not just being out of sorts with a friend or a bad day— assure her that moods come and go. But if she's having a bad mood, the best thing she can do is learn to nurture and take care of herself. Ask her what sounds comforting to her. A back rub? A cup of hot tea? A warm bath? A blanket warmed in the dryer and tucked in around her? A cool rag?

Teaching our daughters to soothe themselves when they are blue is an enormous gift. This is not the time to give lectures on keeping a happy face or you will only add guilt to the pile of emotions already stacked up.

Cramping Her Style

If a woman doesn't become pregnant during her cycle, the lining of the uterus (endometrium) breaks down and hormones are released. These hormones, prostaglandins, tell the muscles of the uterus to squeeze the lining (menstrual blood flow) out. These muscles are the same ones that push a baby out during childbirth, so they are very strong. Some women may have a lot of prostaglandin, which makes their muscles squeeze faster and harder. It's believed that this is why we get cramps.

I never had much pain with my period, but I knew friends in junior high who would cry and have to go to bed with the cramping. Even young girls can experience PMS, cramps, bloating, headaches, backaches, and tender breasts. Hopefully your daughter will soar through her period, but if she does experience discomfort, here are some ideas to help.

Haven't Got Time for the Pain?

There are many ways to help your daughter ease her menstrual cramps, should they bother her. The trick is to find one that works for her.

- Gently rub her abdomen with lotion warmed in a bowl in the microwave.
- Cut back on sugar, salt, and caffeine.
- Give her medication containing ibuprofen.
- Take a multivitamin with iron.
- Encourage her to go to bed or lie on the sofa with a heating pad.
- Eat more fruits, vegetables, cereals, and whole grains.
- Volunteer to run her a hot bath. (My personal favorite. Hot baths cure *everything* in my book.)
- Exercise.

Just for Fun

Cramp-ercize

She is in pain clutching a pillow to her stomach. The last thing in the world she may want to do is move, but exercise will help. It will increase blood and oxygen circulation, helping cramps. Exercise will also help reduce PMS and stress, easing headaches and backaches. Aerobic exercise, when you sweat, will help cut down on bloating. Light exercise during your daughter's period will help to ease the heavy, bloated feeling. Workouts that stretch the body are best to start with.

Here are a few exercises she can try. Get on your stretchy comfy pants and T-shirts together, put on some music she likes, and get ready to . . . *cramp-ercize!*

1. Sit on the floor, legs as far apart as you can get them. Hold your toes if you can, or clasp your ankles lightly. Keep your back straight and breathe in, holding your diaphragm (the muscle under your ribs) up and in. Holding this position, take a few deep breaths. As you breathe out for the last time, bend forward towards the floor and exhale.
2. Sit with your knees open and bent at the sides, with the soles of your feet together in front of you. Clasp your hands under your toes or hold your ankles. Press the soles of your feet together and breathe in, deeply expanding your chest and lifting your diaphragm, as described above. Raise your head a little, and feel your stomach expand. Breathe in and out deeply into your stomach four or five times.
3. Lie on your back with one leg stretched out, and pull the other knee up to your chin. Clasp your knee with your arms to ease the strain and then hold the posture, relaxing for a few minutes.

Medical Treatments for Cramps and PMS

If you've tried all the home treatments and nothing helps, consult your doctor about the medical options available. The doctor can work with your daughter to determine the cause of her discomfort and the best possible solution. What might the doctor diagnose or prescribe?

1. **Hormone Treatments:** Some doctors give patients birth control pills to keep the patient from ovulating. If you don't ovulate, you probably won't get cramps. However, most moms are understandably nervous about putting preteens on birth control pills and the girls might be equally as uncomfortable. This is only suggested if nothing else works, and, of course, they are usually only prescribed for girls in their mid to late teens.

2. **Anti-prostaglandins:** These are drugs that reduce the effect of prostaglandins and a doctor may prescribe them. By reducing hormones the doctor can help vary the cycle and its intensity.

3. **Surgery:** In extreme cases, for example, when severe cramps are caused by endometriosis, a doctor may perform surgery with a laser. Endometriosis is a mysterious, often painful, and disabling condition in which fragments of the lining of the uterus (womb) become embedded, or implanted, elsewhere in the body. An article from the FDA Consumer Magazine reports, "Of the more than 3,000 patients registered with the research program of the International Endometriosis Association in Milwaukee, 41 percent report having symptoms as teenagers. About 5 million American women and girls, some as young as 11, have endometriosis . . ."

   According to the article these girls have terrible pain, maybe six to eight of their twelve menstrual cycles, and often come to the school nurse month after month, needing pain medication or being sent home vomiting, writhing on the floor. One method to remove diseased tissue is for the doctor to use a laser that is connected to a laparoscope and positioned so that its intense light beam is directed through the laparoscope onto the tissue to destroy it. The procedure usually is done without an overnight hospital stay and requires only about a week's recovery time at home.

Rave Reviews

The Body Book by Nancy Rue (Zonderkidz, 2000)

This fun-to-read book has all the "girl stuff" young girls have been dying to know about: everything from puberty to cramps to diet and exercise.

Preparing for Adolescence by Dr. James Dobson (Gospel Light, 1999)

Eight cassettes, perfect for listening to in the car. Focus on the Family's Dr. James Dobson knows how to speak directly and sincerely to adolescents about the topics that trouble them most—like feelings of inferiority, the physical changes of puberty, and much more. His insights, concern, and sincerity quickly win their respect and attention. Available at www.focusonthefamily.org or 1–800–A–Family.

Other Rites — and Riots — of Passage

Buying a First Bra (Or Making Mountains Out of Molehills)

When do you take your daughter bra shopping?

- When she asks for one—no matter how little evidence there is to support

- When you see that she's blossoming and feel that she needs one for modesty

Most girls like to start with sport bras first because they fit snugly and comfortably, almost like a tank top. But you may have a daughter who loves femininity and lace. If so, let her pick out something pretty she'll enjoy wearing. Assure her that breasts come in all sizes—and whatever size hers are, they are perfect for her!

Annette Smith, my friend and author of *Help! My Little Girl's Growing Up*, also suggests that you do something childish and fun on the day you take your daughter to shop for bras: visit the zoo, eat Happy Meals at McDonald's, buy a toy. Let your daughter know that, just because her body is developing, you don't expect her to be *all* grown-up yet.

I also love Annette's rules for clothing that she allows her daughter to wear:

1. It must be appropriate to the occasion. Her daughter has lots of input on this.
2. It must be modest. This is up to Annette and her husband. There is very little, if any, room for negotiation.

A note: It may be necessary to explain to your daughter that what is modest on a six-year-old girl may no longer be modest on a blossoming twelve-year-old girl. It may not be fair, but oh well, that's life.

Smooth Shaver

I'll never forget being in fourth grade—and the first night I shaved my legs. I still have the scar near my ankle to prove it! But boy, was I proud. A shy little girl by nature, I somehow mustered the courage to tell my teacher that I had shaved my very own legs. I'm sure she probably smiled at the large Band-Aid covering my mistake, but I never noticed. All I knew was that I was growing up and I liked it.

You might need to demonstrate how to shave when your daughter asks if she can do this and you feel she is ready to be trusted with a razor. Show her as you shave one strip, then let her try her hand at it. In no time, she'll be a pro. Be sure to use shaving lotion to help get a nice smooth shave. (Mixing a little soap with shaving lotion works really well!)

Clean-up tip: Don't forget to show her how a little shampoo on a washrag does wonders for removing the bathtub line of hair often left after she shaves.

A nice just-because-you-are-growing-up gift for your daughter during this time of her life could be a basket or bag of trial-sized shaving cream for women, a few razor blades (and a couple of Band-Aids), some nice lotion, antiperspirant, facial cleanser to help prevent pimples, a couple of mini pads, flavored lip gloss, a pair of pantyhose, and a bottle of clear nail polish—for her nails, and to help to stop any runs in her new pair of pantyhose. Add any other items you happen to see and think she'd enjoy as she moves into her teen years.

God, Mom, and Me

Jesus Understands Female Emotions

Read Matthew 26:6–10 together. Then read the following excerpt from a Bible commentary.

"Jesus probably had spoken of his coming crucifixion. Mary, kind-hearted, compassionate, thoughtful, lovely Mary, perhaps, noticing a look of pain in his eyes, said to herself, 'This is no parable. He means it.' And she went and got the rarest treasure of her household, and poured it on his head and feet, and wiped them with her hair. Perhaps not a word was said. But he understood. He knew that she was trying to tell him how her heart ached. Jesus appreciated it so much that he said that what she had done would be told of her wherever his name would be carried to the ends of the earth and to the end of time."[3]

This is a story about a woman with a lot of emotion, who came to Jesus with a jar of expensive perfume that represented many months of work. The men around the scene thought this was a big financial waste—an emotional outburst of affection involving very little common sense. But Jesus, knowing the men were whispering about the woman and looking down on her actions, looked a them directly and said, "Why are you bothering this woman? She has done a beautiful thing to me." Talk about standing up for the girl! And later he added even more praise: "Wherever this gospel is preached throughout the world, what she has done will also be told, in memory of her."

How do you think this made Mary feel? Does Jesus understand the way women often think and give with their whole heart?

Absolutely, positively, *yes*. Jesus, unlike human men and boys, completely understands a woman's emotions and loves them!

Assure your daughter that Jesus understands her emotions and loves her because she feels things deeply, even if the boys might tease her about it sometimes.

Memorize the words "It is a beautiful thing she has done to me," and remember that Jesus looks at girls and women and says the same thing to us when we love him with all our heart, soul, and emotions!

---

[3]Henry Halley, *Halley's Bible Handbook* (Zondervan, 1924), p. 501.

chapter five

The Dating Game

Helping Your Daughter Relate to Boys

s any other parent out there stupefied by elementary and junior high kids saying they are "going out" with someone in their class? All I want to know is "where are they going out to"? When I ask this question of my children they look at me as if I'm fresh from having a lobotomy done.

"MUH-ther! They don't *go* anywhere. It's just what they call it these days."

"And they never actually go *out* anywhere together?"

"Nope."

"Do they talk to each other, or sit by each other, or hold hands or anything?" I ask naively.

This question always gets great laughs from my son Gabe. It is obvious that I am a confused old woman, so he explains patiently. "You see, Mom, if a boy likes a girl, he gets his friend to ask the girl's friend if she wants to go out with him. If she tells her friend to tell his friend, yes, then they are going out together. And they don't ever have to talk to each other or nothin' if they don't want to. Then when they get tired of going out, the boy or the girl gives a note to the friend of the other boy or girl saying they don't want to go out with them anymore and that's it! Then they can start all over again."

Duh. Of course! I can be so dense.

If only this long-distance-style romancing remained the norm for our daughters and sons. Alas, there comes the day when our daughters begin growing up, and boys get brave enough to actually talk to them in person—without benefit of a mediator.

Realizing I could not prevent my blossoming teen from the universal experience of The First Crush, I was relieved that her first brush with a real boyfriend was, literally, the boy next door: Josh. To make matters even better, Josh's mom, Melissa, was one of my closest friends.

I found out about their budding romance one morning at 7 A.M., when the ringing phone woke me from a sound sleep.

"Hello?" I said, awake but not fully aware.

"Becky, it's Melissa. Have you heard?"

"Heard what?"

"Our kids are officially boyfriend and girlfriend."

"Rachel and Joshua?"

"Yes!"

"But they've just been buddies, pals, boy and girl next door all these years."

"Well, wake up and smell the romance. Josh has asked her to go with him and she said yes and do you know what that means???"

"What?"

"We could be mothers-in-law someday."

I sat up in bed and blinked to let the vision of our two children in front of a stained glass window focus more clearly in my mind. I could just barely make out Rachel with her golden curls silhouetted by a white lace veil, and Josh, tanned and handsome in a black tuxedo, standing, waiting for his bride. "We could be, couldn't we? Mothers-in-law, I mean."

"Do you think this calls for coffee?"

"Of course! I'll put on the Folgers. Meet me at my kitchen table in twenty minutes."

Within the hour, Melissa and I were sipping at our steaming mugs, munching on bagels, and discussing the futures of our children, grandchildren, and great-grandchildren. The news of our children's recent pairing transformed us from best friends and neighbors (we call ourselves "Lucy and Ethel") into two Yentas. It all felt so Yiddish, sitting across the table, future mothers of the bride and groom. I wished for a scarf and an apron and a thick foreign accent, for I was really in the mood for meddling.

"You know what's really great?" I asked, a comforting thought crossing my mind.

"No, what?" asked Melissa.

"You and I have known each other so long and have been through so much family trauma that the kids know all about our mutual family shortcomings. There'll be no surprises after the honeymoon is over."

"That's right," answered Melissa, brightening at the thought. Then raising one eyebrow, and doing an expert imitation of Freud, she added, "And da dysfunctions ve know are much better dan de dysfunctions ve don't know."

By the time we had planned the wedding, the honeymoon, named the grandbabies, and planned when and where Rach and Josh could spend their holidays, it occurred to us that Rachel was, after all, only fifteen. And Josh, though a fairly mature sixteen, didn't look anywhere near ready to tackle a mortgage on the Victorian house we'd mentally built and decorated (located, of course, equidistant from each mother-in-law).

As it turned out, the courtship of Josh and Rachel was a brief-but-sweet romance. After a summer of selling snowcones and skiing around the lake together, the nip in the autumn air reminded our kids that, after all, they were fifteen and sixteen. Though they cared for each other, neither was ready to call a halt to the pleasures of flirting freely once they started back to school. Rachel cried off and on for twenty-four hours, a ritual all fifteen-year-old girls are allowed to indulge in at the end of a first love. The breakup had been as gentle as possible, both pledging to remain friends. Then with me singing old movie tunes—"Many a new day will dawn . . ." and "I'm gonna wash that man right outta my hair"—in the background, Rachel dried her tears, washed her face, and applied fresh mascara and lip gloss. She slipped on her favorite faded blue jeans and a soft pink sweater, filling them out as only girls in their prime can do. Then she gracefully sailed off to enjoy the other fish in the freshman sea.

Between this first boyfriend and her upcoming actual wedding to Jody the Gorgeous (my terrific son-in-law-to-be), I imagined at least five weddings and grandbabies into and out of existence. To my surprise, as soon as I began warming up to her newest beau and enjoying his presence around the kitchen, she'd break up with him and leave me missing the kid more than she did. One of the more interesting breakups I observed occurred when one of Rachel's boyfriends asked her to return a bracelet he had given her for Christmas. It was a lovely piece of jewelry, studded with tiny birthstones, and both of us were shocked that he had asked her to give back a Christmas present!

However, without missing a beat, she said, "Sure, come and get it." She then went calmly to her room, took a pair of metal cutters and cut the bracelet into several one inch pieces, put the results in a jewelry box, and handed it to him when he came to the door, with a sweet smile. We never heard from that particular young man again.

I couldn't help but be secretly proud of her. In fact, Rachel spent very little time mourning the loss of boyfriends who did not treat her as the precious gift from God she knew herself to be. Her sense of self-worth helped her quickly assess which suitors were gentlemen and which ones were jerks.

And heaven help the boys who turned out to be jerks.

Just for Fun

Rules for Dating My Daughter

Rule One: If you pull into my driveway and honk, you'd better be delivering a package, because you're sure not picking anything up.

Rule Two: In order for us to get to know each other, we should talk about sports, politics, and other issues of the day. Please do not do this. The only information I require from you is an indication of when you expect to have my daughter safely back at my house, and the only word I need from you on this subject is "early."

Rule Three: I have no doubt you are a popular fellow, with many opportunities to date other girls. This is fine with me as long as it is okay with my daughter. Otherwise, once you have gone out with my little girl, you will continue to date no one but her until she is finished with you. If you make her cry, I will make you cry.[4]

The Birds and the Bees Hit the Road

One of the best ways to have the Big Sex Talk in a more natural way is to take a fun road trip alone with your daughter. Head to a quaint or artsy town to go shopping or visit an amusement park—and if possible, design the trip to take about

---

[4]A version of these rules can be found online at members.aol.com/Love4JULI/dad-rules.html.

three hours, one way. There is something about relaxed conversation in a car—stopping for burgers or a picnic at a roadside park—that allows both of you to open up slowly, both going to and coming back from a trip.

You might say something like, "So, when I was about your age I was really curious about what sex was all about. Girls whispered about it, guys joked about it, but it was awhile before I learned the truth about what it was, and why God created such a thing between men and women. You may know more than I think you do, but I'd really like to be the one you can talk to, ask questions of, and trust to tell you the truth. And the first thing I want you to know is that sex is God's idea, and it is absolutely wonderful. But I need to be honest with you: For women to enjoy sex in all its glory, they need to feel safe, loved, protected, and nurtured by someone they absolutely trust will never leave them. God's best is for you to enjoy your first experience with sex with a man who loves you enough to have married you. Lots of girls don't wait until they are safe and snuggled in the arms of their husband before entering into sex, and most of them deeply regret it. They feel cheap and used— as if something precious were given away much too soon."

Let her know why this is so:

1. The first time a young woman has sexual intercourse, she usually experiences more pain than pleasure. Sex, for a woman, takes time and patience—she needs to be relaxed and loved. She needs to feel cherished and safe. Marriage is the best place for this to happen. (As my mom told me, "Guys are usually the only ones who enjoy themselves the first time sex happens in the backseat of a car.")

2. Pregnancy can happen so easily and many girls end up having babies or getting abortions—sometimes after the first time they have intercourse. Giving in

to a moment of temptation can quickly put an end to all the fun of being young and free.

3. If a guy pressures you to have sex, he's probably pressured and been with other girls. This means he may have a sexually transmitted disease, or even AIDS—and give you this unwanted gift that can make your life miserable, or even take your life from you.

As you explain the actual process of sexual intercourse to your daughter, she will probably giggle and that's okay. In truth, the whole thing does sound rather hilarious and an unlikely way for God to bring babies into this world. Especially to a young girl's mind! Laugh a little along with her, and then let her ask questions. Tell her the truth, without shame, using clinical words for body parts—but also talk about the emotional and spiritual meaning for lovemaking between husband and wife. The symbol of a woman opening to her husband, being vulnerable, and allowing him to fill her body with a part of himself is a beautiful picture of the two becoming one flesh. Sex is fun, for sure, after some time and practice with a committed husband! But it is also a sacred joining—a blending of bodies that God created to bring pleasure, and children, into our lives.

The Dating Progression

Many young people are looking for creative alternatives to the typical dating scene popularized by Josh Harris's runaway best-seller, *I Kissed Dating Goodbye*.

To simply avoid dating altogether is one possibility worth examining, and courtship dating is also gaining popularity, but most young people balk at the thought. If you decide to allow your daughter to date, a good way to deal with dating is to make it an earned process. Talk to your daughter ahead of time about the timing and stages of dating in your household.

Here's what we used in our home:

1. **Junior High:** Group outings or "dates" with a boy only
   if his mom, dad, or family comes along too. Emphasis on church and school youth excursions. Some of
   Rachel's first dates were with a young boy from a His-
   panic family. It was the perfect situation since they
   traveled in a clan. A vanload of mama, papa, grandmother, siblings, and cousins would drive up to take
   Rachel to church or a movie, or over to their house
   for menudo stew and a family video. She found their
   unique family culture fun, cozy, and fascinating.
2. **Age 15–16:** Double dating with another trusted
   couple. (It is especially nice if the other couple
   includes an older brother. Big brothers generally do a
   great job of watching out for little sister.) At this
   point, the boy needs to come over to the house to get
   to know our family first. Robert Wolgemuth, who
   wrote the book *She Calls Me Daddy*, insists on prein-
   terviewing any young man who wants to date his
   daughters. He talks about how precious she is and
   how he expects his daughter to be treated on a date,
   when to bring her home, and what to do if they find
   themselves unavoidably running late.

   Make sure your daughter has a cell phone with
   her and keeps it on so that she can call you or you
   can call her at any point in time.
3. **Age 16 and up:** If, and only if, your daughter has
   proven herself trustworthy, you may want to allow
   her to go on a car date alone at this age, but only
   with a "preinterviewed" young man. Take this in
   stages as well—allowing for the first dates to be
   short, returning home before dark. If that goes well,
   allow her a little more freedom and a later curfew
   as time goes on.

Pulling on the Reins

One spring, Rachel broke her curfew two times in a row, and began acting in ways that concerned her father and me. We did some detective work (calling the parent network) and found out she'd been to a party we'd forbidden her to attend. The following day, her father and I told Rachel how much we loved her, and that we believed she was making some poor choices. "So," I said, "I will be your new best friend for the summer." She could not believe we were grounding her from dating for the entire summer, but she would tell you today that this was the best decision we ever made.

In July, our delicate, feminine daughter was bored enough to agree to go with a church youth group on a hiking excursion in Colorado. She went up that mountain a sullen teen, she came down it, a couple of weeks later, having begun to blossom into

Rave Reviews

Check out www.truelovewaits.com to find out information about books, events, conversations, and tapes for teens who are committing to wait until marriage for sex.

The Princess and the Kiss: A Story of God's Gift of Purity by Jennie Bishop (Warner Press, 2000)

This is a wonderfully illustrated children's book that transcends all ages because it is written in allegory form. Mothers are reading this, raving about it, and giving it to their daughters from ages two to twenty.

Maximum Dating (audio tape) and *Maximum Dating/ Love/Sex* (video series) by Josh McDowell

These are attention-holding, positive, enthusiastic, and convincing messages that every teen needs to hear to hold out for God's absolute best in dating and marriage. Available at www.josh.org or call 972–907–1000.

a confident young woman with a faith, and sore feet, both tested to the limit. Naturally shy, Rachel found courage within her to join this group even though she did not know a soul. Many of the girls on that trip became fast friends. She later talked about what an advantage it was to join a group that had no preconceptions about her. She was free to be the best version of herself—and found she really liked that person.

Never hesitate to pull the reins if you see your daughter swinging out of control. But don't just send her to her room and ground her. This only brings resentment and little positive change. Instead, good-naturedly become her "new best friend"—take her fun places, talk with her, teach her new skills (good time to show her how to make that pie crust from scratch), let her know you care. She'll balk at first. Ignore this. The pouting stage is generally short-lived if you let it roll off your back and continue on with the game plan. Encourage her to join in healthy adventures or to take up a new hobby. This is a good time to learn to play the guitar, join a choir, take art lessons, or go on a mission trip.

How to Attract the Right Guys

Here is advice I've given young girls through the years when it comes to getting the right kind of boy's attention.

1. **Be yourself.** Don't pretend to be someone you aren't to attract a boy. It's too much work and you can't keep it up forever.
2. **Learn the art of give-and-take conversation.** A good conversation is like batting a tennis ball back and forth. Get a book of interesting questions to have on hand—questions that require more than a yes or no answer. For example, "What's the happiest memory you have from your childhood?"

3. **Dress attractively but avoid looking cheap.** Sure, guys will stare at the girls with low-cut blouses and shorts the size of washrags—but they will also stare at a train wreck. You want to be seen as "classy" not "trashy." To be respected and admired as a person of inner and outer beauty is so much more satisfying than being ogled like an object.

4. **Let your presence say, "There you are!" instead of "Here I am!"** Be happy to see others, enter into their world before starting in with a long story about yourself.

5. **Be a little mysterious.** Girls who put their heart on their sleeves right away with boys tend to scare them away. There's an art to showing interest in a nice boy, and yet leaving them wondering a bit, wanting to be with you again. Don't tell them everything about you at once, but allow relationships to unfold slowly.

6. **Be interesting and use humor.** Get interested in life—astronomy, reading, rock climbing, music, gourmet cooking—and others will be drawn to the passion your enthusiasm generates. Laugh often, but never at another person's expense.

Chick Chat

Ask your daughter to give you three good questions that she might use to help start a conversation with a boy. For fun, you pretend to be the guy and answer her questions as you think a boy her age might answer. This is a good way to weed out those too-easy-to-answer questions that only require one word. Then reverse it—you ask questions and let her be the "guy." Have fun with this, and don't hesitate to use humorous or outrageous questions and answers.

7. **Spread the joy around!** Don't pair off and leave your friends behind. They'll resent it, and besides, your boyfriend needs to know that he is not the center of your universe.

8. **Make God your #1 priority** and let any boy that wants to date you know it. You can be good friends with lots of guys, but only date the ones who share your faith.

9. **Just say no.** Don't be afraid to say a confident no to any boy who pressures you to do anything you feel violates your standards. If he doesn't respect you, you don't need to be with him.

10. **Set standards before you ever go out on a date.** What sort of touching is allowed and when? Talk this over with a trusted youth director or parent or older Christian girl you admire. Handholding? Letting a guy put his arm around you? Kissing? The truth is, holding hands can be enormously pleasurable for a very long time if you tell your boyfriend that this is as far as he can go with you. I just spoke with a man in his forties who is about to marry a lovely woman. With the joy of fresh love in his voice, he confessed, "Becky, simply holding her hand is the most sensuous thing in the world." My philosophy on this is to enjoy and *prolong* the stages of touching in dating. Squeeze all the joy out of simply holding hands. You have a long wait until marriage, in most cases. Take it slow and save petting and sex for your wedding night. Value your far-off, future, husband-to-be enough to give him something brand new to unwrap after you are married!

God, Mom, and Me

Read the following scriptures together:

- 1 Corinthians 6:13, "Our bodies were not made for sexual immorality. They were made for the Lord, and the Lord cares about our bodies."
- 1 Corinthians 6:18, "Run away from sexual sin! No other sin so clearly affects the body as this one does. For sexual immorality is a sin against your own body" (NLT).

So many people—in movies and on TV—don't make a big deal about having sex with others before marriage. What does God say?

Why and how does sexual sin affect the body?

Why does God ask us to save this wonderful, fun, and holy activity for marriage?

What are some ways you can keep yourself from temptation to sin in this way? Encourage your daughter to write these down. She will need a plan in place ahead of time, before she gets in a situation where her feelings could begin to take over her convictions.

chapter six

In Search of Kindred Spirits

Knowing the Importance of Friends in Your Daughter's Life

Today Rachel and I looked at wedding dresses, talking of what her bridal colors would be. (Lavender, seafoam green, antique rose, and ivory—colors not found in most men's palettes or vocabularies.) Then we talked about who her bridesmaids would be. Of course there was no doubt in my mind, but I wanted to hear her name them. I smiled and nodded as she said, "Cricket, Michelle, Amber, and Kari—they've been my friends since kindergarten." And they mean the world to her.

During the girls' sophomore year in high school, Rachel received a call that Cricket, Amber, and Kari had been hit head-on by a car on a busy highway near our home. Amber was thrown from the car. The woman who hit them died, either on impact or of a heart attack beforehand.

Miraculously, they found tiny Amber, face down in a ditch—and other than a few minor injuries, she was whole, healthy, and intact. Cricket and Kari were also relatively unharmed considering the enormity of the accident.

Rachel, with tears streaming, went straight to the hospital and sat vigil over her three dear friends all night.

Even before this brush with death they have survived so much together—heartaches and heartthrobs, the first day of school and their first dates—but then, what lifelong friends haven't?

I recently turned the pages in my writing notebook to a piece I wrote in 1996, the year my daughter was twelve. Today I am looking at a beautiful bride-to-be and her lovely attendants; it seems like yesterday I was riding herd over five bobbing heads in braces and braids in my living room.

July 1996:

I can no longer remember what my daughter's right ear looks like. As far as I know, she may not even have one anymore. The ear has been undercover, hiding incognito, beneath a telephone receiver for at least the last ten months. Not only that, but the telephone cord has transformed into Rachel's umbilical cord—transmitting all the information needed to sustain life in junior high school.

Another interesting phenomena: I only see my daughter these days as part of a pair. She's always with one of her best friends—usually, Michelle (whom Scott lovingly nicknamed, Miss Prissy) or Cricket (whom Scott insists on calling Grasshopper). I try not to look at the situation as if I've lost a daughter, but rather, as if I've gained a revolving set of twins.

It's imperative, of course, that Rachel and her girl friends keep up-to-the-minute on the details of every aspect of each other's lives. The following are halves of actual conversations I've heard from Rachel's end of the phone chatter.

"That zit hasn't cleared up? Ohmygosh, how *awful!*"

"He did? He said he liked me? Liked me, like, LIKED me, or liked me, like, *likes* me?"

"Oh, yeah! I spilt Dr. Pepper on my Nikes—WHAT?"

"DID I NOT TELL YOU THAT?"

"He's the guy that threw a french fry at me in the cafeteria and then I giggled like a dork and milk started spurting out my nose and I, like, thought I would DIE! You know—he's the one that used to go out with Chelsea, and just broke up with Heather, and I think he's really fine but I don't just know for sure, for *sure* if I'd go out with him or not."

One thing is for sure: Rachel and I are not so very far apart when it comes to girl talk. This weekend three of my old girlfriends and I gathered in Dallas and rented a hotel suite for a night. We arrived about 5:00 in the evening and talked and giggled until 2 A.M., slept a few hours, rose again at 8:30 the next morning, and continued nonstop chatter until noon— when we practically pried ourselves away. There were still stories untold, discussions left hanging, questions unanswered. My stomach, three days later, is still sore from hours of laughing.

"What in the world did you girls talk about for thirteen straight hours?!?" Scott asked in amazement when I arrived back home.

"Oh, I don't know . . ." I said, "First, I guess, we told our 'cute kid' stories. Brenda told about how she'd bought her little Ben a one-minute timer and told him to brush his teeth until the sand ran out of the hour glass. The next time she passed by the bathroom, Ben had thick foam all around his mouth, dripping down his chin, his shoulder, and down his right arm. Bless his heart, turns out Brenda gave him a *three-minute* timer. And then Shawn told about her four-year-old decorating the floor of her car, parked in the driveway, with hundreds of doodle bugs while she was napping."

"And this kind of stuff really entertains you girls?"

"We love it!"

"Did you talk about any current events or anything?" Scott asked, trying hard to understand.

"Of course. We discussed nutrition. Did you know that Cabbage Diet gave someone an ulcer? We decided that diet must work by putting a hole in your stomach so the food can leak out. Then after we finished discussing all the diets we'd been on, we ate a ton of chocolate."

"I guess I'll never understand women," he said before heading out the back door.

What I didn't tell Scott was that eventually our Girl Talk turned deeper: we talked of ongoing quests to find our purpose in life, what it means to really know God, to be real. We each wondered if we'd ever overcome the pain of our imperfections as women, mothers, and wives. How could we learn to forgive more, holler less, love our families better? Women do this talking thing really, really well. Connectors R Us.

What woman doesn't understand Anne of Green Gables longing: "I've dreamed of meeting her all my life . . . a bosom friend—an intimate friend, you know—a really kindred spirit to whom I can confide my inmost soul"? No place is really home to a young girl or a grown woman until she has another friend she can call up on the phone for no reason at all.

Since friendships are such an enormous part of your daughter's life, let's explore why this is so, and how you, as the mom, can enhance her ability to make and keep friends.

Why Boys Don't Do Chick Chat

According to Dee Brestin's book *The Friendships of Women*, "The friendships between little girls differ from the friendships between little boys." She also points out that perhaps it is not always such a terrible thing, this lack of deep conversation between the males of our species. Some of it may just be a built-in difference between the sexes. Brestin goes on to quote

Zick Rubin, author of *Children's Friendships*, as saying, "Girls not only have a much stronger need for friendship than boys, but demand an intensity in those friendships that boys *prefer living without*." (Emphasis mine.)

Perhaps you have observed this difference in your family. Though my husband and my sons value their friends, they've got to be doing something in order to talk. Conversation is "by the way"—and rarely the main course. None of my three sons ever called to find out what color socks his buddy was going to wear to school the next day. There were no long chats between the males in our family over hairstyles and the latest school gossip. Hurt feelings between the boys and their friends were almost never a topic of dinner conversation. And frankly, they didn't seem to miss or need this heart-level communication.

Our daughters, however, are in training for womanhood and honing friendships that will, hopefully, stay her over a lifetime. Just as women friends have sustained and nourished her mother, her grandmother, and her great-grandmother before her.

It Takes a Village — Of Friends

In my book *Coffee Cup Friendship and Cheesecake Fun*, about friendships between women, I wrote, "From *Little Women* to *Steel Magnolias*, I'm drawn to stories centered on female group bonding. I think this is because I know, from personal experience, that it takes a variety of friends, each uniquely gifted, to bring a rich wholeness to life. I imagine we are all jigsaw puzzles with little parts of us missing: small flaws, things we don't do very well (organize, cook, remember birthdays), or places where we hurt and need comfort or an infusion of another's joy.

"Then a certain friend comes along and fits into that little open place, making our life more complete and suddenly we realize how much we'd been missing that connection, that little puzzle piece in human form."

One of the reasons I believe girls tend to move in groups is because women like a variety of personalities to choose from! One way to help your daughter prevent herself from devastating hurt if a friendship goes awry is to encourage her not to put all her friendship efforts in just one other friend's basket. In the above book, I describe all types of friends that I thoroughly enjoy—all of them unique, and I love them for a variety of reasons. I have chapters on my favorite "Chick Flick Friends" and "Can Do Friends," "Entrepreneurial Friends" and "Playful Friends," "Bookworm Friends" and "Atta' Girl Friends"—each woman bringing God-given gifts into my days. (And I hope I bring something to them. Not a home-cooked meal or organizational help. But maybe a little levity.)

Encourage your daughter to reach out to more than just one best friend, even though that one most special friendship may always feel as comfortable as an old, soft robe. Like the old Girl Scout song that's been sung around campfires for decades says: "Make new friends and keep the old—one is silver and the other is gold."

She'll be better emotionally cushioned if she has both.

Chick Chat

Tell your daughter about your grade-school friends. What did you usually play at recess? Ask your daughter about her friends and what she likes best about each one.

Reach Out and Touch Someone

The other day my sister and I were talking about the values our mother passed down to us—and one of them that we most appreciate is the way she taught us (more by example than lecture) to walk into a room and immediately focus our attention on others. So that our presence might say, "There you are!" rather than "Here I am!"

In addition she taught us to be compassionate to the loners and shy ones in any given group, something that takes a lot of focused effort for kids. How did she do it? She'd say things like, "Honey you have such a sparkling personality—and I couldn't help but notice how nice you were to that shy little girl at the party today." In other words, she gave us *lots* of strokes for any movements toward compassion and an attitude of reaching out.

When my kids would go to church camp, rather than talking about the possibility of them being homesick and how much I'd miss them, I followed my mother's lead and would tell them, "Now you kids have been given so many talents and friends. Would you do something for me this week? Would you look for one boy or girl who seems a little down, and you can tell feels left out—and just make their week happier by including them and speaking kindly to them?"

They might hem and haw a little bit, but inevitably, when I picked them up at the end of the week, they had a story to share about how they helped another child feel better in some small way.

Five Ways to Encourage Your Daughter to Make New Friends

1. Talk with your daughter about girls she is interested in knowing better. Call the girls' mothers, introduce yourself, and ask if you might take the girls on an outing (lunch, a movie, shopping).
2. Encourage your daughter to be involved in sports or other classes or ventures that use her gifts and talents. Team efforts and interactive classes are a great way to meet several new friends.
3. Organize a party or "game night." It doesn't have to be elaborate. Make phone calls and invite several girls

(and moms or parents if you wish) to come to your home for party games or board games.

4. Whenever you learn of someone who is new to the neighborhood or school, take the initiative to introduce yourself and your daughter to the new girl on the block. If a child has just made a move, they are usually desperate for at least one acquaintance who will be a familiar face, and possibly a new friend.

5. Partner with the other mothers of your daughter's friends. This is important so that all the mothers can be on the "same page" about acceptable movies, social activities, etc. By the time the girls are teens, they have friends (and you'll have other parental support) who are all standing together on driving rules, dating, and so forth.

Special Considerations

The Shy Child

One way of helping your daughter be less hesitant to make friends is to give her an "icebreaker" toy or activity to introduce into a situation. Active toys like jump ropes or sidewalk chalk or even a simple ball can entice other children into play. Don't force her to be more social than she wants to be; if she seems reluctant give her some time until she begins feeling comfortable. Keep working on building confidence at home and in situations where she is confident.

The One and Only

Only children tend to gravitate to older children because they are mostly in the company of adults. They are often very mature, confident, and organized. However, they can also tend to gravitate toward children much younger than they are because they can call all the shots. It's especially important for you to encourage only children to make friends with other kids of the same age to learn those sharing and negotiating skills.

The Over-Achieving Child

Some children try too hard to make friends with everyone, and actually stress out if any child in their class doesn't like them. You can help by sharing what therapist and author Cynthia Spell Humbert calls the 20–60–20 Rule. Cynthia says, "Twenty percent of the people you meet will just 'click' with your personality and you'll know this right away. Sixty percent of the people you meet are in the neutral category—you don't especially like or dislike them. They are just there. Then twenty percent of the people you meet will grate on you like fingernails on a chalkboard." By sharing this with your child, she will realize that if only twenty percent of the kids in the class like her a lot—that is great. And she doesn't have to feel internal pressure to like everyone she meets either.

Be a Second Mom — Determine to Love Your Kids' Friends

We say yes way more often than no (9–1) to our kids' requests to have a friend, or group of friends, over to spend the night, to have an impromptu party, or to have dinner with us. (Or, more realistically, to make a run to a fast-food restaurant with us!) Recently a mother was dropping her child off at our house for one of these last-minute Saturday night parties, and she asked me how I could stand all the kids and the noise.

For one, I have to admit, my personality type (sanguine) can handle quite a bit of chaos around me as long as everyone is having fun. Secondly, I don't clean the house when my children choose to have a party—they do. (Parties are highly motivating to them.) And I don't sweat it if there is dust on the furniture and smudges on the floor. Your children's friends do not care, trust me. They also know they are totally responsible for the clean-up after the party's over.

We have a two-story house, and if you are entering the teen zone and considering a new house, there are huge bonuses to having an upstairs area for kids. It cuts down on the noise and I don't see the mess. Since Scott built our second story, I have completely stopped griping at my kids for their messy rooms. I almost never see them, and what I don't see doesn't bother me.

My kids (along with a friend or two) also plan the party menu within a given budget (they know where to buy the cheapest pizzas that will fill up a hungry crowd)—or they call and ask everyone to bring certain items. (Always ask specific kids to bring specific items. If you say, "Bring anything!" they usually come with hands full of popped air.)

Be the Carpool Queen

It doesn't take much to impress kids. When they climb in your car to be transported to the next ball game or school event, try to ask each child a question and give them a compliment. "What a cool shirt!" "Man, you shot a great basketball game last night." "How did you get so good at math?" This models conversational skills for them.

Laugh and be cheerful. They love nerdy moms who are joyful, even if they tease you playfully. Here's a recent quote from my fifteen-year-old son: "Mom, you are the worst driver in the carpool. You drive like an old woman. But I have to hand it to you, you are always in a good mood and I'd rather go slow with a happy mom than go fast with a grumpy one."

Take Advantage of the Moment

Sometimes, on the way to our local Brookshires or Wal-Mart store, with Gabe in tow, we'll stop by and pick up a friend to take along, just to go grocery shopping with us. I let them play a couple of video games and get a cheap soft drink from the machine, and if they help me load and unload the groceries, we drive through Taco Bell or McDonald's on the way home.

If you make your home and your car (which, for several years running *might as well* be your home) lots of fun, you will encourage other kids to come along and in turn, help your child become more sociable.

Though my Rachel is now very outgoing and poised, for years she was painfully shy and soft spoken—terrified to move or speak out of her comfort zone. But the more we had her little friends in our home, the more Rachel "caught" the joy of reaching out to others and being liked in return.

Consider Staying Put If Possible

If your children are doing well in the school they are in and have good-quality friends—especially after fourth or fifth grade—carefully count the cost before moving them away from

Just for Fun

Naming Them Two By Two

Give your daughter's friends cute little nicknames. I had a teacher in third grade who called us all her "little beasties." My father often referred to a gaggle of kids as "sproogins." My husband got a kick out of taking a child's name and pretending to get mixed up and calling them some funny variation of their real name. Our own kids have nicknames but we also bestow them to our children's best buddies who frequent our home often. Thus, Rachel's friend Cricket became "Grasshopper" at our house and our house only. There's a friend of Zach's I always affectionately called "Giraffe," and right now, for the life of me, I can't think of his real name! What can I say? It's a zoo around here!

a great friend-school environment. Sometimes a move simply cannot be helped, but as your children get older and especially into junior high and high school, don't fix what ain't broke—unless you absolutely have to. Peers are so influential at this time—a handful of positive friends at school, church, or in the neighborhood may be worth a lot more, long term, than moving for a better job with a raise.

(My sister, whose husband was without a job for a very unnerving year, wanted to add that if you are out of work and a job is offered you across the country—and it's the only job available—take the money and move. Your kids will get over it in therapy.)

Chick Chat

Inevitably there will be the day—perhaps many of them—when your daughter will burst into tears in your arms, crying because one of her friends hurt her feelings or snubbed her. Friends can be wonderful, but how they can wound one another at this age. (My mother often said, "Junior high girls can be carnivorous—eating each other alive with their words.")

What to do? Just love on her. Tell her that you understand how much she hurts, and that feeling rejected is one of the most painful human emotions for all of us—young and old alike. More than likely, these situations work themselves out—and the next day or two she'll come home smiling and chatting with the news that she and her best friend "made up."

Remind her at this time that Jesus will be the only friend she will ever have who will never hurt her and always love her and keep her best interest at heart. These are times to draw near to him together in prayer, and perhaps to encourage her to pour her heart out in a prayer or poem or journal on paper. (You might even buy her a pretty journal just for this purpose.)

Move Your Daughter if She Lands in Trouble City

On the other hand, don't wait too long to change your child's situation if you can see her consistently making poor choices in peers (drugs, gangs, etc.) or if she shows signs of being constantly ridiculed or rejected. Do everything you can to help her adjust to her school or a church group—and give her some time to do that. But if you see that she is either always hurting or getting into trouble, consider moving your daughter (or son, for that matter!) to a different school, enrolling her in a private school, or even home schooling for a while. Sometimes a move from one area of the country to another or a different city is just what a family needs to begin a new adventure and help a troubled teen turn over a new leaf where she won't be pre-labeled.

Youth Groups Are Worth Their Weight in Gold

All four of our children spent some time in youth groups and enjoyed a church camping, mountain hiking, or summer mission trip experience. Each of their lives was dramatically affected in extremely positive ways. Two of my children found youth groups they loved, two others have struggled with youth groups at church—but found Christian friends at school they bonded with.

A Mom of Influence

What a ministry you can have, moms, just by sitting and listening to your friend's kids at the kitchen table as you pour them a cool drink, or work a puzzle and chat casually together. Though our oldest son graduated from high school four years ago, his friends still call us and come by to see us. In fact, I just said goodbye a few minutes ago to one of Zach's buddies who is about to graduate from college, get married, and go on to medical school. He stopped by just to say hello and let us know how well he is doing—and get the earful of kudos and encouragement he knows he can expect from us. The other day my son told a friend of mine, "My friends love Mom like a second mother!" At first I thought he sounded a little perturbed, then I saw there was real pride around the edges of his grin.

Rave Reviews

"If I Really Wanted to Be a Great Friend I Would . . ." by my sister, Rachel St. John-Gilbert (River Oak Publishing, 2000)

This little book is fun to read, filled with hints and ideas that your daughter can read and try for herself. At $5.00 it's a real bargain!

201 Questions to Ask Your Kids/Parents by Pepper Schwartz, Ph.D. (Avon Books, 2000)

This is a cute, creative, practical book to help the budding friendship between you and your daughter. If you read the book one direction it is filled with questions that you can ask your child. Going the other direction, there are questions your daughter can ask you. Keep this book, or any good book of questions (check Half Price Bookstore) in the glove compartment and bring it out to make terrific use of the wait at traffic lights or train crossings.

Lily and the Creep (fun fiction) and *The Buddy Book* (illustrated, informative) by Nancy Rue (Zonderkidz, 2001)

In the Young Women of Faith series, these are companion books that deal with friendships among girls.

Signing Off with Girl Talk

I just got off the phone a few minutes ago with a good friend. She said, "Becky, I just made a decision. I need you to tell me that I'm doing the right thing." I listened to her story and answered her with exactly what she wanted to hear. "Absolutely. You are doing the right thing." (A man, you see, might want to point out miscellaneous logical options. This, of course, only confuses and angers a woman.) "Thanks," my friend answered, audibly relieved, "that's all I needed to know."

After I hung up, Scott casually asked what the call was about. I answered, "You wouldn't understand. It was girl talk."

Then I went on to discuss the conversation with the only other person in this family who *would* understand—my daughter, Rachel.

God, Mom, and Me

Write out the word *friend* as an acrostic. Then write the following words that describe some of the attributes of good friends. Look up the verses and talk about what each word means.

F–Faithful, Hebrews 3:2

R–Refreshing, Acts 27:3

I–Instructful, Acts 18:25

E–Excellent, Daniel 5:12

N–Neighborly, Matthew 5:43

D–Doer, James 1:25

Give your daughter a tiny Bible or cross to keep in her purse or pocket at school. Every time she feels lonely or left out, remind her that God goes with her everywhere.

Beyond Burgers, Malls, and Rock 'n' Roll

Helping Your Daughter Appreciate the Classical Arts

had this terrific idea to drive Rachel on her twelfth birthday from our country home to the big city of Dallas and a lovely mother-daughter tea room, complete with big frou-frou hats. But first, we'd drop off at my favorite spot in the world: Barnes and Noble Bookstore, where I would allow her to spend a $15 gift certificate on any soul-enriching, heart-lifting book she wanted to buy. I just knew she would love it!

We drove an hour and a half to Big D on her big day. We arrived at Barnes and Noble and just as I settled into my favorite book section, Rachel arrived at my elbow, looking slightly bored. She definitely had that "When are you goin' to be done, so we can go" look about her eyes. But she held off on complaining because she knew this was my big treat to her.

I glanced at the small bundle in Rachel's outstretched arms. She had picked out three teen mysteries in fifteen minutes and was delighted to have that part of this mother-daughter birthday trip done.

Ah, well . . . there was still the Tea Room.

Or maybe not.

As we walked out of the bookstore toward the car, Rachel piped up, rather nervously. "Mom, could we possibly just drive through McDonald's for Chicken McNuggets 'cause that's what I'm really hungry for and I kinda want to get home and see what Cricket's up to . . ."

I had one of those major Big Mother Choices. I could insist Rachel spend her birthday the way I dreamed it would be, or let her have her day and enjoy it from a twelve-year-old perspective.

I passed the test. I let go of my preconceived expectations with a quiet, internal, inaudible sigh. Then I laughed and pointed the hood of my car toward the Golden Arches, where we enjoyed lukewarm trapezoids of preformed chicken—in an atmosphere of relaxed celebration.

But later, as I thought over the day, celebrated her way, I wondered where I might have gone wrong. Perhaps I had waited a little long before trying to introduce Rachel to the classical, artsy, gourmet side of life. We had raised her in the country, where the height of fine dining was the new Applebee's out on I–30. (Why do I suddenly feel like a character in one of Jeff Foxworthy's books? You know you're a redneck when your daughter asks to do a drive-thru for her birthday dinner.)

Thankfully, as Rachel matured she acquired a taste for some classical music—very little, softly playing in the background. She and her best friends actually went to Dallas to eat at a lovely restaurant during recent holidays, then saw the *Nutcracker* ballet together. So there's hope that her life won't be one nonstop series of dinner in a bag or bucket.

Still, I thought it might be best for this chapter on introducing your daughter to the fine arts to get some help from another mother who actually raised her daughter on the milk of Mozart and Michelangelo instead of Chicken McNuggets and McGraw (Tim, of course), who played Pachelbel for her daughter as I drove mine through Taco Bell.

This might be the *Mom's Everything Book*, but trust me, I'm certainly not the mom who knows everything. But I do know where to find the moms who know how to do what I don't do all that well! (Isn't that what friends are for?)

Appreciation for "Culcha"

I am blessed by friends who are also creative writers, lovers of the fine arts, and mothers of daughters. I asked if I could interview Lynn Morrisey for this chapter because, frankly, she's done an exceptional job of helping her daughter foster what will be a lifelong love of classical art, music, reading, writing, and dance. I wanted Lynn to share her secrets of what really works with us. Lynn is founder of Noteworthy Living, author of *Seasons of a Woman's Heart*, and an inspirational speaker.

Her only daughter, Sheridan, was born to her rather late in life—and Lynn has done a masterful job of raising Sheridan to enjoy the creative arts, beginning from the womb! (Or as my sister, Rachel, says, employing her best New Jersey accent: "That Lynni has given her daughter lotsa cul-cha.")

Becky: *Lynn, describe what giving our children a taste of "culture" means to you.*

Lynn: When I think of children, I automatically think of treasures because Scripture teaches that children are a gift and reward. I love to consider my lovely daughter, Sheridan, as one so valuable that she is a pearl in the making.

A cultured pearl is one that is made on purpose. Just so, our children can be trained *on purpose* to appreciate culture and beauty in their surroundings. It doesn't happen by osmosis—they must be trained; but with a little forethought and creativity, it is easier than imagined.

Just as a cultured pearl is formed layer upon layer in the oyster shell, consider wrapping your child in "layers of culture"—layers simply wrapped around everyday activities, starting from conception—layers that become a natural part of their environment and experience.

Enjoying the Art from the Start

Becky: *You were a real lover of the arts, music, and dance before you had a child. How did you feel, at age forty, when you discovered you were pregnant?*

Lynn: I thought my adult life was over. I hadn't planned on having a child and didn't relish entering the world of babydom. God changed my bad attitude, giving me tremendous love for my little angel and desire to teach her. I soon discovered that I did not have to roll up and die because I was a mother; rather, I took my daughter to my usual artsy haunts and introduced my world to hers.

Becky: *How did you do that?*

Lynn: I never went to McDonald's, I left that to her dad. I learned quickly that I could take Sheridan to quasi-fine restaurants where children were permitted and that offered children's entrees. These were wonderful "laboratories" in which to teach Sheridan etiquette, using *their* props, like linen napkins and nice

Just for Fun

Plan a special, inexpensive tea party in your own home or work with other moms to put on the ritz for your little girls around your own kitchen table. Emilie Barnes has some wonderful books for moms and little girls on how to host tea parties. For extra fun, the girls can wear big floppy hats and bring their favorite doll or stuffed animal.

cutlery. Many fine hotels and tea rooms have special programs in which children are encouraged to dress up, drink cocoa out of fine china, and eat cookies and tea cakes in luxurious surroundings, sporting their best manners. Since she was two and a half, I have taken Sheridan to the Ritz Carlton for their annual Teddy Bear Christmas Tea.

Becky: *Lynn, I know you love to read as much as I do—both of us could be happy in Barnes and Noble for a week. Has Sheridan caught the reading bug from you?*

Lynn: Absolutely! My husband, Michael, and I started reading to Sheridan in utero and, upon her arrival, continued this nurturing practice. Rather than just baby books, we read actual Scripture passages (especially the psalms) or children's poetry written by great poets, rather than strictly nursery rhymes. This practice introduces children to a varied vocabulary and rich imagery. Her favorite poetry books include *A Child's Garden of Verses* by Robert Louis Stevenson, *Poetry for Young People* by Carl Sandburg, and *The Children's Treasury of Classic Poetry* (Barnes and Noble Books), which includes such gifted poets as William Blake, Gerard Manley Hopkins, Henry Wadsworth Longfellow, William Shakespeare, Christina Rossetti, and Emily Dickinson.

Michael and I also encourage her to write her own poetry, and her favorite subject is her dog, Bogey. This enhances her personal creativity, makes her more aware of her own world, and causes her to dig deep into her vocabulary to try to discover rhyming words.

Becky: *My kids loved poetry as well, especially poetry with some humorous twists.* Where the Sidewalk Ends *by Shel Silverstein was a favorite and one by Judith Viorst,* If I Were in Charge of the World, *were two of the most dog-eared books in the Freeman kid library.*

What other books would you recommend to moms and daughters?

Lynn: Rather than just reading "kids" books, encourage your daughter to read books like the Great Illustrated Classics series (Baronet Books)—child's versions of classical literature such as *Little Women, Heidi, Black Beauty, Tom Sawyer,* and *The Secret Garden.* In this way she can experience great literature on a child-friendly level, and that may spur her on to read the "real thing" at a later date.

I would also recommend *Honey for a Child's Heart* by Gladys Hunt, which offers a definitive suggested reading list of good children's literature. Another great way to introduce children to good literature is to attend children's book readings at libraries or bookstores. These events are typically free.

Becky: *Brenda Waggoner's beautiful book for women,* Storybook Mentors, *is the perfect book for moms to read as they reintroduce (or read for the first time!) old classics like the ones you mentioned to their daughters. It has the lovely look and feel of a children's book, complete with color artwork inside—but it is written for us grown-up girls.*

Chick Chat

Bring out your daughter's artistic and intellectual interests by asking the following questions:

- What are your favorite subjects at school?
- If you were a grown-up and had a little shop, what kind of shop would you want to own?
- What is your favorite musical instrument to listen to? Is there one you'd like to learn to play?

Artsy Are Us

Becky: *Okay, we've covered fine dining, literature—what about introducing our daughters to art?*

Lynn: While I am no artist, I do appreciate beautiful art and, despite my lack of talent, have been able to introduce it to Sheridan. Since she was an infant in a stroller, I have taken her to the St. Louis Art Museum (also free!). Even at an early age, she was enthralled with the paintings' brilliant colors and interesting textures and shapes. While children's art classes are available for a nominal fee, often Sheridan and I simply ask to use a portable folding chair, bring our own pads and pencils, and sit in the various galleries and sketch. Art museum staff grant permission as long as you are quiet and refrain from touching the paintings. It is a wonderful "up close and personal" way in which to introduce children to art, while encouraging their own creativity, as well.

In addition, instead of decorating her nursery and now "big girl room" with typical Disney cartoon characters, bright balloons, and the like, Sheridan's walls are adorned with tasteful art prints or Manuscriptures by well-known Christian artist Jonathan Blocher. These are beautiful calligraphed Scripture verses adorned with some type of illustration.

Music and Dance

Becky: *What about music appreciation? Any thoughts?*

Lynn: Studies have shown that babies hear in the womb. I began singing art songs and playing classical piano music for Sheridan before she was even born. Once she was here, I put her to bed, wrapped in snuggly blankets and the soothing strains of classical lullabies—for example, Johannes Brahms' *Lullaby and Goodnight*, Mozart's *Lullaby*, William Byrd's *Lullaby, My Sweet Little Baby*, or Engelbert Humperdinck's opera *Hansel and Gretel*. Bach and Pachelbel are also good choices.

One need not know how to sing or play an instrument in order to teach appreciation for good music. If performing is not your forte, there is a wide variety of professionally recorded

Rave Reviews

One of the best places I've found for children to see and touch art is in beautifully illustrated children's books. There was a PBS special on children's book illustrator Tasha Tudor my daughter and I found fascinating. Tasha is a tiny sprite of an older woman who has chosen to live the "Little House on the Prairie" style—as in olden days. We love reading Tasha's books and the books about her life from the local library. I finally bought the video *Take Joy!* because it was such fun to watch this childlike woman cooking on a wood stove, tending her garden, painting by firelight and sunlight, and creating puppet shows and miniature doll houses. She even had a tiny mailbox on her daughter's door and, as I recall, Tasha would write tiny notes from imaginary "doll" friends and leave them in the mailbox for her. (See www.tashatudorandfamily.com for more information.)

music from which to choose. Consider playing classical music on a regular basis in your home. It is a painless way to gradually introduce your child to this exquisite art form. Research also shows that children who listen to Mozart or Bach find it easier to concentrate on homework.

Becky: *Now that's motivating! What is your view of taking children to live performances?*

Lynn: I would recommend that you attend child-friendly classical concerts. Many churches offer free concert series at which children are welcome. In the summertime, my husband and I would attend free symphony concerts in the park. We'd bring a picnic dinner, blanket, and our young daughter. No one seemed to mind if she was fidgety in this casual setting. Such excursions were excellent "practice" for attending concerts at our symphony hall. In the beginning, we made sure that we sat near an exit, and usually only stayed for the first half of the performance. By sneaking out during intermission, we left before the point of no return when Sheridan might become sleepy or antsy. Now, at nine, she enjoys listening to entire performances.

There are professional concerts geared just for children at symphony halls, such as Tchaikovsky's *Nutcracker* ballet or *Peter and the Wolf.* Often such concerts are preceded by lectures by the conductor, encouraging children's questions and comments. Each Christmas, we take Sheridan to a Bach Society concert, where she can participate in audience caroling during the candlelight processional. The joy radiating from her face testifies to her love of beautiful music. Of course, caroling around the neighborhood or enjoying family sing-alongs around the piano or to a recording are excellent ways to introduce your children to music.

Becky: *Music takes on new life for our kids when they not only listen to it—but find themselves performing music! I loved acting and singing in the school musicals* Li'l Abner *and* The Music Man, *and my husband made a convincing Rabbi in his high school production of* Fiddler on the Roof. *What great memories we have of those times.*

Lynn: Oh, yes! Don't miss opportunities for your children to perform, such as in a church or school choir, school band or orchestra, or Vacation Bible School and church pageants. Often no auditions or professional lessons are required. It's a great way to expose your children to the excitement of participating in live musical events.

If these opportunities are not available or if your budget precludes attendance at the symphony, realize that many musical performances are available on videotape. Since she was very small, Sheridan has loved watching concerts with Luciano Pavarotti (her favorite tenor in the womb, as well!), the Vienna Boys' Choir, the *Nutcracker* ballet or *any* ballet featuring Mikhail Baryshnikov, another of her favorite performers, and lately, Charlotte Church, and the operas *La Boheme, Carmen,* and *La Traviata.* In my opinion, some scenes are too intense for a young child, and so I skip over them.

The Walt Disney classic *Fantasia* is an excellent movie whose rich, colorful, and imaginative animation brings heart-stopping classical music to life. Interestingly, when Sheridan and I recently attended *Nutcracker,* she recognized the music as coming from *Fantasia.* While she transposed the two, not realizing that Disney had borrowed from Tchaikovsky, it made me aware just how easily she recognized the music itself.

Becky: *Lynn, thank you so much for your wonderful thoughts and ideas. Had I known you when my daughter was younger, I would have probably been inspired to reach for more opportunities to share the arts with my child—and maybe a few less french fries! Of course, it's never too late. I wonder if my eighteen-year-old Rachel might be up for some Beethoven, crumpets, and tea.*

God, Mom, and Me

> I have been reminded of your sincere faith, which first lived in your grandmother Lois and in your mother Eunice and, I am persuaded, now lives in you also. For this reason I remind you to fan into flame the gift of God.
>
> 2 Timothy 1:5, 6

What an influence moms and grandmothers have on their kids!

What God-given gifts do you see in your daughter that you'd like to help fan into a flame? After reading the above verses together, tell your daughter that you'd love to support her in pursuing any gifts and talents she has, or areas that she wants to explore and learn about.

Share the following quote from the movie *Chariots of Fire:* "I feel God's pleasure when I run." This is one of the best ways we know that we are using a God-given gift. When we are engaged in this activity, we feel joy bubbling up inside, and often we find it comes especially easy to us, it's natural. I once heard a preacher ask, "What does Jesus see through your unique eyes?" It's exciting to think about how he enables each one of us to do something unique for his glory, something that will uplift others.

On a piece of paper, both of you write the sentence "I feel God's pleasure when I . . ." Both of you list five things you do that gives you each a sense of bubbly joy inside. Then list five things you each dream of doing or learning about—a skill or an experience—before she graduates from high school. Put the paper in a special place to be reread on her graduation day and see how far you both will have come. By identifying with her (showing her that this "old dog" of a mom can still learn new tricks), you'll encourage her by example.

Finally, read Ecclesiastes 11:6: "Sow your seed in the morning, and at evening let not your hands be idle, for you do not know which will succeed, whether this or that, or whether both will do equally well." Encourage your daughter to "scatter her seeds broadly"—to try a lot of things while she's young because she won't know what she is gifted at if she doesn't try many activities. Who knows which adventure "seed" might grow into a lifetime passion?

── c h a p t e r   e i g h t ──

What a Wonderful World

Helping Your Daughter Become a Lifelong Learner

This New Year's Eve my daughter and her new fiancé, Jody; Gabe and his fifteen-year-old girlfriend, Allison; along with my husband, Scott, and I, brought in the new year together. At the stroke of midnight, we poured small champagne glasses of nonalcoholic bubbly and toasted one another in the kitchen as the radio played "Auld Lang Syne" in the background. The song that played next turned out to be one of my absolute favorites.

It was Louis Armstrong's laid-back, jazzy tune of gratitude: "What a Wonderful World" (I call it an Optimist's Ballad). Without saying a word, each couple sat their glasses down on the table, took their respective sweetheart into their arms, and began dancing to the old classic song about what a wonderful world we've been given to see, feel, touch, and experience. Trees of green, red roses in bloom, skies of blue, clouds of white, colors in the rainbow—and "on the faces of people passing by"—affection between friends, a baby's cry. What an incredible world God has given us to learn about and explore!

During the first week I taught first grade, I had my children take this song and illustrate each phrase of it. I wanted them to begin their journey through first grade with a sense of awe, wonder, and gratitude at the world around them—and how much fun we were going to have exploring it together.

You may not see yourself as a teacher, but you are the most influential educator your child will ever know. To help your child become a lifelong learner, to inspire her curiosity about all there is to learn and discover—is an incredible gift you can give your daughter.

Not only do we mothers have great opportunities to help our daughters explore and love the arts, we will also have ample opportunity to help them get excited about any subject they might learn in school. How? By making what they learn in the classroom practical and *fun* at home and in everyday life.

There is no way I could list the thousands of ways you can have fun learning with your child, and encourage her to do well in school and in life, but here are some ideas to get you started.

Geography and Social Studies

I bought two huge laminated maps to display in my office at home: one of the world, and one of the United States. (You can purchase them at an office supply or teacher store.) I refer to them all the time since I travel to speaking engagements, but I never dreamed how much my kids would also enjoy them. Be sure to have a globe on hand somewhere too—even a cheap blow-up globe ball will work (and double as a beach ball in a pinch).

As you learn about various countries and cities—by watching movies, videos, and reading historical, biographical, or geographical library books—have your daughter put a sticker on the places she most wants to visit someday. You might even plan a special mother-daughter trip upon her graduation from high school—somewhere she has researched and is longing to go. You could start collecting your pocket change in a big jar for this, with the words "Our Dream Trip" written across the front. It will heighten the anticipation and make the trip seem even more special.

Put a different color of sticker or pushpin in places anyone in your family has traveled to.

Let your daughter collect travel folders of various states, cities, and countries that she visits or wants to learn about. You can find fascinating information by visiting a travel agency or by typing a city or country in the keyword section of your Internet search engine.

Here are a few great places for kids to learn geography on the Internet:

- www.nationalgeographic.com
- www.orbigo.com (interactive map games)
- www.edu4kids.com (practice remembering state facts)

No Longer Directionally Challenged

One of my favorite memories was traveling to a family reunion with Rachel when she was ten, just us girls in the front and her little brother in the backseat. For this special occasion we even rented a little red sports car at a bargain price for the weekend. I purposely put Rachel in charge of the map and she loved it. I had only recently realized the freedom I felt when I learned to read maps—forced to do so when I had to land in new cities and drive rental cars around. I wanted Rachel to experience the self-confidence of knowing she could find her way around the country to anywhere she wanted to go—with nothing but a little know-how and a map.

I like to think that because of that fun trip, where I dubbed her "The Navigator," Rachel has never been intimidated by maps or directions as I was for so many years! A compass on the car dashboard is a marvelous tool and will help your daughter realize that north is not always the direction she is looking at with her geography book in her lap. Line her up with "true north" every so often as you are driving or walking or observing the stars.

I taught my students the four directions by singing a song I made up. First I pointed them toward north in our classroom (you can do the same in her bedroom, even labeling the walls). Then we'd sing, "North is just in front of your nose, south is behind your head and your toes. Raise your right hand toward the morning light, that is east—what a beautiful sight. Now raise your left hand, it's pointing west—these are the directions that I like best!"

Chick Chat

Ask where your daughter wants to go on family vacation this year and let her be a part of the planning. Look at a map and allow her to trace the shortest route to take. Ask her to do some Internet or library research and make a list of things she wants to see and do on the trip.

Cooking around the World

One fun way to explore the world without leaving home is to cook recipes from around the world. Have an Italian night, or a Mexican fiesta! It is also fun to visit ethnic restaurants, beyond Chinese and Mexican food, if your budget allows it. Try

Thai noodles or Ethiopian sponge bread at unusual ethnic restaurants found in most large cities.

You could also invite over foreign students and have them tell about their culture. Or, if your daughter has friends from another cultural, ethnic, or religious tradition, invite them over for a special tea. One mother I know gave a tea for her daughter's tennis team. Most of the little girls were Jewish or Catholic and were to come prepared to share their favorite holiday family tradition. After each girl told her family's tradition, her daughter was able to share their Advent tradition with her friends. It was a wonderful opportunity for friendship evangelism.

History

Probably the best way to get interested in history is to start with a great biography or historical movie. Once your daughter finds herself interested in one person or character (real or fictional) she will become interested in the surroundings and time period almost *by the way*. When she learns about the colonial period from her history books, she might have already read a biography of Betsy Ross—or an American Girl book about a girl her own age during this time period. History will take on life!

Abby, Lost at Sea by Pamela Walls is the first book in a wonderful page-turner adventure series for girls ages eight to twelve that will introduce them to the exotic South Sea Islands. I read portions of this book aloud on a children's radio show and found myself reading the entire book because I wanted to see how it ended! Any of Laura Ingalls Wilder's books or the American Girls series will show your daughters our American culture during several different periods in our nation's past.

There are great biographies for girls on so many interesting women: Helen Keller and her teacher, Annie Sullivan;

Florence Nightingale; Juliette Gordon Lowe (founder of the Girl Scouts); Betsy Ross; Harriet Tubman; Madame Curie; and many others. Don't forget biographies of women in our modern history: Wouldn't you like to know if Julia Child made gourmet mud pies as a child?

Lois Lowry has a gift for creating memorable young heroines set in historical periods. In her book *Number the Stars*, set in Denmark in World War II, Annemarie hides her Jewish best friend, Ellen Rosen, and embarks on a heroic mission to save her life. The Orphan Train series is another favorite, set in the Old West, when orphans from cities were sent to pioneering families by train.

Grace Products has some of the best "visual biographies" I have ever seen for kids in this eight to twelve age group. Reg Grant, a professor at Dallas Seminary, a true Renaissance man, plays the old librarian who takes kids back in time to view a historical event in this series of professional, high-quality videos. All of my children, various ages, boys and girls, thoroughly enjoyed these videos (1–800–527–4014).

A great read for moms is a book called *Moms Who Rocked the World* by Lindsey O'Conner. Lindsey combines her writing skills to create a fiction, time-travel, and factual history novel that brings women in history, like Susannah Wesley, alive to modern mothers.

One of the best ways to bring history alive is to read a book (or listen to a tape or CD) about a certain period of time, then travel to the actual setting of the event, or visit a museum. My friend and editor Bucky Rosenbaum lives in historic Nashville and every year there is a reenactment of a scene from the Civil War—at the actual sight of the battle. As I recall, the drama begins in a cemetery and the actors pop up from behind the tombstone under which the person they are portraying was buried. (Talk about holding a kid's attention!)

Fort Worth, Texas, has a Log Cabin Village where kids can try their hand at spinning wool or dipping candles—and many cities have these places close by. Williamsburg, Virginia, is a favorite historic location for families to see colonial history come alive.

We once hosted an Old Fashioned Day in our country neighborhood that will always be remembered as one of the most fun days our children ever enjoyed. In one part of the backyard my builder husband, Scott, dressed like Ol' Abe, and erected a log cabin playhouse. My sister-in-law set up her quilting frame in the front yard and the neighbor across the street brought her horse to give the children rides. There was bread making in the house and candle making on the front porch and guitar playing by the barn. We gave the children twenty minutes at each location then rang a bell and they moved on. We wound up the day with a potluck picnic and hand-cranked homemade ice cream. Everyone was tired, but the weather was perfect, and a feeling of contentment was pervasive. As we watched the sun set and the children having a ball, the grown-ups—used to running off to work with briefcases and waving at each other—got a taste of old-time front porch sittin' and visiting.

Now *that* was a history lesson—for all of us.

Practical Math

I love this anecdote that came in by email from my friend Judy Baker and her daughter who just didn't "get" math:

My daughter and I had always shared a love of reading and writing, which warmed my heart and gave us many pleasant hours together. Unfortunately, we also shared an equal disdain and ineptitude for all things mathematical. Upon being introduced to basic algebra, she came home from school highly indignant. "Mom, you're not going to believe this," she said waving her math book in the air.

"They want us to mix letters with numbers. Well, I'm not doing it!"

Subjecting her sacred letters to associating with the numeric enemy was equivalent to having angels sing in hell. True to her word, she didn't do it. I know because I drove her to summer school sessions at 8 A.M. four mornings a week.

Ahh . . . even with all the modern emphasis on math and science for girls, moms and their daughters still tend to confess to more math anxiety than do their dads and brothers. Rather than argue about why this is, I have found it more helpful to do what you can to make math make sense in everyday life to your daughter.

Use everyday opportunities to use the math that you know she is learning in school at home. When she is studying geometry, think of some way she can apply it to her life. Let's say she wants to paint her room. Can she figure out how many square feet she needs to cover the walls? Give her the price per gallon of paint and tell her how many square feet the paint will cover. Let her figure out how many gallons she'd need and how much it would cost to paint her room. Let her dream of new carpet—how many square yards would she need to cover her room? Let her look at carpet prices and figure out the approximate total cost of new carpet for her bedroom.

When you teach your daughter to cook using measuring cups and spoons, take a moment to look in the front or back of a good cookbook (the old red and white Betty Crocker is great) for the Table of Equivalent Measurements. It will tell you, for example, that there are sixteen tablespoons in one cup and three teaspoons in one tablespoon. Have her become familiar with these as she learns to cook. Then sit down with her one day with a couple of recipes in hand—and, using what she knows about math and fractions, have her double the recipe.

Then triple it. And so forth. Pizzas and pies give other opportunities to divide and conquer the concept of fractions.

Use your trips to the grocery store to teach math. Gallon milk cartons, pints of cottage cheese, quarts of orange juice, and a liter of cola provide visual measurements for your daughter to observe. As you are shopping for groceries, ask her things like how many quarts of orange juice could fit in one gallon of milk.

Store coupons and clothing sales are great ways to help your daughter learn percentages. Can you teach her how to figure out what 30 percent off of a $25 skirt would be?

Finally, sewing or scrapbooking can provide opportunities to use rulers and measurements on a small scale.

Rave Reviews

The Magic School Bus Series by Joanna Cole (Scholastic Trade)

With its wacky teacher Ms. Frizzle and adventuresome bus, this series is highly recommended for engaging kids in all sorts of scientific exploration—from studying space to under the sea, under the ground, or inside caves! Available at most public libraries and children's bookstores. I used these books as often as possible when teaching children about the earth. The humor and interesting little pictures and charts make this series enjoyable learning at any age.

The Glad Scientist Series by Karol Ladd (Holman Bible)

Four books filled with exciting experiments which teach about God through the science lessons. Topics include meeting the Creator, visiting outer space, exploring the human body, and learning about the weather. You can purchase these in a set and save money on Karol's website at www.karolladd.com.

Nature and Science

Vegetable or flower gardens are great fun and not only teach your daughter the joy of planting and watching something grow, but she can observe science in her own backyard! You can often find large seed packets designed specifically for children's gardens with giant sunflowers and directions for how to grow green bean teepees and a nice variety of easy-to-grow edibles.

You can even plant sweet potatoes (with eyes) in a cup of water and produce a nice green vine across the kitchen or bedroom windowsill. And presoaked beans in a paper cup are still as fun to watch sprout as they were when you were in school.

Sprouts are like instant plants and much fun to grow because you can eat them in just a few days. Buy sprout seeds at the health food store along with the jars to rinse them in. Or you can use zip-lock bags with holes poked in the bottom (with a toothpick) to drain the water as you rinse the seeds each day. My kids like sprout, peanut butter, and banana sandwiches!

Buy or borrow some pocket guides to birds or plants. Go hiking in nature and see what you can identify together. Make a nature journal of your discoveries.

Fill a net bag (like the kind that fruit comes in) with bits of cloth, dried grass, yarn, dryer lint, or cotton. Hang the bag outside and watch the birds pull out what they need to build their nests.

After visiting a planetarium or reading a book on the constellations, go outside on warm, clear nights and look at the stars and find the Big Dipper, the Little Dipper, and so on.

A friend of mine who lost her husband makes a regular habit of going outside, blanket spread on the ground, to look at the stars. She and her boys talk about their daddy together during these times and how he might be looking down at them from heaven. When I visited her, the boys started begging to look at the stars as soon as the sun went down!

Just for Fun

Kitchen Experiments
Raisin Bobbing

Put three raisins in a clear cup of fizzy 7 Up (or other clear soft drink) and observe them bob up and down. Ask your daughter why the raisins float up and then back down, and up again. (Answer: The bubbles form around the crevices of the raisins and these air bubbles rise to the top of the cup. When the raisins reach the top of the cup, the air bubbles burst and the raisins sink until the process starts all over again.)

Mad Scientist "Gloop"

This is a fun "ooze" to make, touch, and play with!

Ingredients:
8 oz. bottle household glue
Big bowl
Small bowl
1 cup water
Poster paint in several colors
1 cup warm water
2 tsp. Borax powder

Directions:
Squeeze the whole bottle of glue into the big bowl. Fill the empty glue bottle with the water and add it to the glue. Stir well. Add several drops of paint. Mix the warm water and Borax powder in the small bowl and stir. Don't worry if you can't get all of the clumps to disappear. Stirring constantly, carefully pour the Borax mixture into the glue mixture. Stir with your hands until the goop forms globs and oozes easily from your hands.

TIP: If any goop gets on your clothes, wash it out immediately with soap and water.

Sportin' a Fit Way of Life

What are some ways to encourage your daughter to start and stay with physical education and sports?

Remember, girls just want to have fun! Be sure that the atmosphere is one that encourages the fun and joy of the game, working with team members, and watching her skills improve, rather than focusing on the win-lose record.

Encourage her to try a variety of sports while she's young, and eventually she'll find the sport where she naturally shines. Do all you can to encourage in these areas by practicing or playing with her (if you can!), attending games, and cheering her on. If she's especially talented, you might even consider hiring a private coach for a short time or sending her to a special sports camp.

Sports teach her about people and life: Your daughter will learn much about getting along and cooperating with people if she is involved in any sort of team sport. She will learn how to lose gracefully, the rules of good sportsmanship, and how to help and rely on her teammates. These things are not always taught as well in the regular classroom situation.

Give your girl the opportunity to try sports she can do alone (snowskiing, jogging, gymnastics, golf, dancing), sports where group cooperation is essential (basketball, volleyball), and a sport where only two people are needed (tennis, rock climbing). Some girls are very athletic but do not perform as well in groups, and some cannot get motivated without a group of players around them. Some prefer to play with just one friend or opponent.

Compliment your daughter's increasing strength and firming muscles as she exercises and tones her body by playing and enjoying sports. Tell her how proud you are that she's doing something healthy for her body and her mind and emotions. (As we saw in the chapter on emotions, exercise is like Prozac for PMS episodes!)

Don't underestimate the sidelines. Rachel joined team sports at school and though she rarely got to play in a game (basketball was not her best sport!), she had a great attitude about it and always worked hard. She told me she just liked cheering on the other girls and that working out and practicing kept her feeling fit. We laugh good naturedly about the time she complained to her coach of her one sports injury—her neck and back were aching from sitting on the bench so much. She also liked the way she looked in uniform; it made her feel athletic and part of the team of the girls she's grown up with. She loved running, however, and did a great job on the track team.

I recall reading about a little girl who was so excited about her part in the school play. Her mom asked what she'd been chosen to do and the little girl excitedly said, "I've been chosen to clap and cheer!" Being a cheerleader for the team, even if she cheers from the bench, is such a valuable lesson for life— and if she is practicing with the team, she is staying in shape and having fun.

Music

There are few things as relaxing and good for the soul as playing an instrument or singing. My parents insisted each of us learn to play one musical instrument, so we had to take at least one year of lessons. I only took one year of piano, but that year has given me a lifetime of fun as I plunk out pop tune harmonies and easy hymns. My parents had beautiful voices and often sang duets in the car as we drove on trips (and sometimes us kids would offer to give them a nickel to cut it out). I have memories of them singing through entire musicals, often followed by hymns—in rich harmony. My mother grew up in a denomination where there were no musical instruments. Though she now believes God loves the sound of instruments in worship, the one great advantage to not having accompaniment was that everyone in the church knew how to sing in four-part harmony—the result was beautiful. I have wonderful memories of family reunions where uncles, aunts, and my grandmother would break into gorgeous song. Because my mom had one sister and five brothers, each of them took their places as a bass, tenor, alto, and soprano. I learned how to sing harmony to any song simply by family osmosis.

I also had a rare and wonderful youth director, Dean Dykstra, in junior high. He gave all of us who wanted to learn, guitar lessons on Saturday afternoons. I have incredible memories of sitting on the grass cross-legged with a circle of kids as we each strummed and plucked our guitars along with Dean. The result was that he created his own "worship" team for Sunday morning praise singing and Wednesday night youth group. If you, or someone in your church, knows how to play the guitar and is willing to teach it, it is a wonderful way to bond with kids and give them a lifelong gift to enjoy and use for God's glory.

I loved choir at school and participated in every school musical with gusto, as well as several other performing ensembles from dancing and singing in an all-girl group to traveling internationally in college with a madrigal group. I can say without hesitation that my very best memories of my school years involve the field trips, camaraderie, and sheer joy of performance in these musical activities. My children attended a smaller school, where each of them played in the band—and had a ball. I'll never forget my son Zeke's senior year when he came out on stage with two of his best buddies, wearing a white suit and sunglasses, twirling and dancing as he played his saxophone, Blues Brothers style. Because we are also an impromptu dancing family, I was not surprised when he put the saxophone down—held out his hand, and his girlfriend (now his wife), Amy, jumped down from the bleachers and into his arms. They are incredible swing dancers and the two of them jitterbugged like crazy to the wild delight of the crowd. What memories!

On graduation from Zeke's high school, traditionally a song is played as each kid goes out into the audience and hands his mother a rose. Only my son pulled me out of the crowd instead and danced with me to the song "I Will Remember You"—as we had often done when I taught him to waltz or two-step in the kitchen before a school dance. There was not a dry eye in our family. Such is the way music, dance, and song can enrich life's moments with your children. So, moms, take advantage of every moment to enrich your child's life with the joy of participating in music. It is a gift they will always cherish.

Art

If you or anyone in your circle of friends and family has a talent for painting, sculpting, drawing, or pottery making, encourage them to let your daughter watch them at their task, and to teach her some "tricks of the trade." My mother-in-law taught many of her grandchildren the special techniques of watercolor painting. It became the favorite "grandma and me" activity—with a project the two of them could work on together every time they visited her.

My neighbor Mary Sue had an entire craft room built just for the purpose of allowing her and her grandchildren to be creative together. She often invited my own children to join in the fun, and they would come home proudly carrying their latest creation: a whistle made from clay, a mosaic stepping stone, a hand-painted plate. You don't have to be as elaborate as Mary Sue—just create a craft corner somewhere, or a craft box. Fill it with items you can use to make any number of artistic creations with your daughter.

One summer, I took art lessons with my best friend, Allison, who lived across the street from us. My family was musical, but Allison's family was filled with artists. Her mother always seemed to be doing some toll painting on some piece of pretty wood at her kitchen table. Her father worked at home carving and making pieces of wood and craft items. In fact, her mother owned an art supply store. What fun we had with her father's scraps of wood and her mother's paint box!

Be open to any opportunity to encourage your daughter to enjoy the arts—buy her a sketchbook, take her along to a craft store, import "grandmas" and other women to share their artistic talent with her.

A Word about Overload

Before your child ends up doing so many extracurricular activities that she needs to carry a day planner (and you spend your life in the car going to and fro), ask yourselves, *If my daughter adds this activity to her life*

> *will she have ample time for homework?*
> *will it affect family or church related activities?*
> *will it interfere with the private time she needs to rest and relax at home or time with friends?*

Make a list of priorities. Have your daughter list all the things she'd like to do, if she had unlimited time and energy. Then get realistic and choose one or two per semester. Often she can try a new activity next semester or sports season.

If you find that your daughter is sleepy, or slipping in grades, or just generally cranky, reconsider her activities. We know how easily we moms pile too much into our lives; our children are capable of doing exactly the same thing—only they may not realize they need to back off and slow down.

Study Smarter, Not Harder

If your daughter is struggling with a subject and you cannot help her, ask around and find someone who happens to be great at the subject to help her right away. Often a fellow student is the best help, because they know exactly what the teacher is teaching. Don't drag your feet on this; get her back on track as soon as possible.

Assure your daughter that studying in small amounts of time over a period of days, with rest in between, is the best way to retain material. Five minutes of studying a day for five days is always better than cramming an hour the day before the test—even though you've actually spent *less* overall time studying. A little bit every day adds up.

Learn the tricks of the memory trade. If you have ever participated in Walk Through the Bible classes or listened to someone on an infomercial teach you how to memorize long lists of facts, they teach the same method. They associate and create word pictures in their mind, because our minds think in pictures.

For example, let's say your daughter needs to know that the state bird of Texas is the mockingbird, the pecan tree is the state tree, and the bluebonnet is the state flower. Have her imagine the shape of Texas in her mind, then encourage her to make up the most outrageous, moving picture she can with the other three items on top of the shape of Texas in her mind. For example, she might see the mockingbird flying around with a granny's blue bonnet tied around its head. The bird could then land on a tree branch—that is oddly shaped like pecan pie.

Remember to make your picture wild and crazy—your brain will recall it easier. Also, if you can put "action" into the picture, you will have a better chance of keeping the items in your head. Practice the above technique by playing the game where you put several odd items on a table from a grocery bag or box. Using the above technique, ask your daughter to try to remember all the items on the table. Then put them away where she can't see them, and ask her to write down everything on the table that she remembers. Practice makes perfect and this little memory device has saved many students at test time.

Another time-tested way to learn something is to teach it. Tell your daughter to pretend she is teaching a room full of stuffed animals or dolls how to multiply fractions or write a good paragraph. If she can actually talk out loud and pretend she is teaching something, her retention of that information will double. You know the old saying, We teach what we most need to learn. Sometimes we have to *pretend* to teach to learn!

Teacher–Parent Relations

Encourage your daughter, in any subject, to talk to the teacher as soon as she starts getting that "foggy, I'm lost" kind of feeling. Math, especially, is cumulative and once the teacher moves on, it may be hard for her to catch up. Teachers are often most receptive to students after class or after school. If the teacher seems extremely busy, your child can leave a note on her desk politely asking when and how she might be able to get some help for a subject she's struggling with. If this brings no response, you will need to call and kindly inform the teacher that your child is in need of some extra help and ask how you can best get it for her.

Having been on both sides of the teacher desk, I can say that starting every conversation with a compliment on a positive note is usually a great way to begin. Tell the teacher what she is doing right first.

When you describe the problem your child is having, make sure that you don't cast blame on the teacher. Approach it with curiosity, looking for solutions, not blame. "I wonder how you and I might work together to help Kari learn her multiplication tables. Any ideas or resources? I'm pulling my hair out at home."

If the problem is with the teacher's treatment of your child, say, "Lori may be extra sensitive right now, but could you help me think of some ways that you might help her feel more confident and happy and less afraid of making mistakes in your classroom?"

Send your child's teacher an occasional "Atta Girl" note, thanking her for the good things she is doing for children. It is a tough job. Ask her what small items she has to replenish with her own money for use in the classroom: award stickers, snacks for the kids, sticky notes, etc.

She will appreciate being given the things that she often has to buy out of her own teacher's salary, as classroom budgets for "extras" are usually very small. Sometimes a teacher gets only $50 for such things to last her a whole year! A subscription to a special teaching idea magazine or a gift certificate to a local teacher store are much appreciated.

Hassle-Free Homework

A good rule of thumb is that your daughter can come in after school and rest, have a snack, read, or play outside and unwind for a bit. But there can be no TV or video games until homework is done.

Encourage your daughter to make good use of free time to study and do homework at school. The more she gets done at school, the more time there is to play!

If you find homework assignments are eating up all of your daughter's extra playtime, or your family time, talk to the teacher about possibly cutting back on the amount of homework she is sending home. Your child needs time to unwind from the long day of sitting in a desk to go run and play!

In addition, we have found having a small open hanging file holder on the kitchen counter works great for sorting and signing school papers. Every member of the family has a file where he or she can put any papers that need to be seen or signed by Mom or Dad, and Mom or Dad can put them in the child's file when they have signed and read the report.

God, Mom, and Me

Read these verses and ask your daughter the questions about Daniel and his friends:

Daniel 1:17—"To these four young men God gave knowledge and understanding of all kinds of literature and learning."

Where does knowledge and understanding come from? What are your favorite subjects? Which ones seem easiest for you? Do you ever think that your abilities to think and reason and learn are gifts from God?

In one of Daniel's prayers he prays, "Praise be to the name of God for ever and ever; wisdom and power are his. He changes times and seasons; he sets up kings and deposes them. He gives wisdom to the wise and knowledge to the discerning. He reveals deep and hidden things; he knows what lies in darkness, and light dwells with him" (Daniel 2:20–22).

Have you ever wanted to know an answer to a puzzling situation? You have all the knowledge and all of the facts, but still, you don't know what to do, what God wants. This is when you are searching for wisdom, and it goes much deeper than knowledge.

Read James 1:5 for what to do if you need some wisdom. Look up the word "wisdom" in a dictionary and then the word "knowledge" and talk about the difference between the two.

Pretty soon, the king hears about Daniel—not only how skilled he is in book learning, but about his wisdom. Read Daniel 5:13–31.

What are some differences you observe between Daniel and the two kings mentioned in this passage?

What are we to do with gifts of learning, knowledge, and wisdom?

chapter nine

Homemaking 911

Helping Your Daughter Create a Home of Beauty, Love, and Laughter

To open this chapter on homemaking skills, I thought, in the interest of complete and fair disclosure, it would be a good idea to reprint the following story. It first appeared just before Thanksgiving in *Home Life* magazine.

Our children are frantic. Thanksgiving is upon us, and this year I've volunteered to host the event at our home, including stuffing and cooking the turkey and setting an actual cloth-covered table with non-disposable dinnerware.

My seventeen-year-old daughter, Rachel, upon discovering this fact, sat me down in the living room, and in her most maternal tone of voice asked, "Mom, do you really think you're

Chick Chat

Share memories of your childhood home with your daughter. What was your room like? How was it decorated? What could you see out the window?

mature enough to handle a major holiday that involves actual food preparation?"

From the synchronized nodding of her younger brother's head I have been forced to admit, with some sense of shock, that my own children are afraid to trust me alone with a frozen Butterball.

"Not to worry," I continue to reassure them. "I know what I'm doing."

And so, come Thanksgiving morning, I will attempt— heaven help us—to baste with the best of 'em.

I'm putting on a brave front, but truth be told, my family has some reason for concern.

As long as I can remember, our smoke alarm has served as our family dinner bell. When our now-married son, Zeke, was five years old, I handed him a perfectly brown piece of toast one morning. Without batting an eyelash, the little guy took the toast, along with his dinner knife, walked to the trashcan and automatically started scraping it.

"Zeke, honey," I said cheerfully, "you don't have to scrape your toast today. Mommy didn't burn it!"

"Oh," he said thoughtfully, glancing down at the toast in surprise. "I thought we always have to whittle our toast."

The tradition of serving blackened food would continue in the Freeman kitchen for many more years. When Zachary, my eldest son, was about thirteen years old, I recall pulling some nondescript charred casserole out of the oven one evening. The alarm was bellowing, the kitchen soon filled with the familiar fog of fresh smoke. As I sat the casserole down on

the counter and brushed a damp lock of hair from my fore-
head, Zach nonchalantly strolled through the kitchen, put his
arm around me, and said, "Mmm, mmm, mmm. Smells like
Mom's home cooking!"

A few months ago, Gabe was home from school with a
head cold. I took a notion to fry up some bacon for breakfast,
so I plopped the bacon in a skillet and set it on the burner
(turned to medium high). It was a chilly morning, and soon I
got another notion: to take a hot bath to warm myself up. So
I immediately retired to the bathroom for a nice long soak. If
Gabe had not been home and seen the first few flames leap-
ing from the skillet, my kitchen would have, literally, gone up
in smoke.

My problem, I've deduced, is not that I'm a bad cook. It's
just that I'm easily distracted. I'm sort of like a middle-aged
toddler who finds herself totally fascinated and absorbed with
the next new activity—leaving the last activity (i.e., putting
something in the oven) erased from all memory.

I've often wondered if my children have grown so accustomed to overcooked food through the years that they might
accidentally mistake the charcoal for the chicken at someone
else's outdoor barbecue.

This past May, a magazine writer sent a photographer down
to our house to take pictures of our family enjoying a "typical"
Sunday afternoon backyard picnic. I gently explained to the
journalist that the sort of food I normally prepare probably
shouldn't be photographed except, perhaps, for reading audi-
ences with especially strong stomachs. Surgeons and zookeep-
ers might be okay.

"Not to worry," she said, "we'll hire a professional to come
over to your house to cook, decorate the table, and style the
food."

"Wow," I said. "That sounds like a *deal*."

And so it came to pass that by the time Jim, the photographer from Chicago, showed up at my door, a professional food stylist and friend, Jane Jarrell, had miraculously turned my backyard picnic table into a *Southern Living*-ish spread. There were fresh wild flowers in hues of bright purple, orange, and yellow peeking merrily over tops of tall galvanized buckets. Straw place mats that looked like watermelon halves held hot pink and green watermelon plates and bright green glasses and utensils. Fresh ripe strawberries and watermelon chunks overflowed from two clear glass bowls in the center of the table, festooned by heaping plates of barbecue beef, baked beans, a mustard-spiked potato salad, and asparagus pasta. A peach cobbler bubbled away in the oven, its vanilla and cinnamon fragrance tantalizing us even though it was inside the house.

My family took one look at the feast, another longing look toward Jane, then turned to me and asked, "Mom, can we keep her? Huh? Please?"

Sadly, Jane had to return to her own family at that point, but I assured Jim, and my family, that I felt sure I could carry out any remaining hostessing duties solo.

"Do you make up the stories about the crazy things you do in your books?" Jim asked at one point between snapping pictures of my family deliriously stuffing their faces with Jane's fabulous food.

I shrugged. "So far, to tell you the truth, Jim, I haven't had to make up any stories. Weird stuff happens to me almost every day. It's like material manna from heaven."

Still, I noticed that Jim looked slightly unconvinced.

The afternoon wore on and Jim asked to take pictures down by the dock on the lake where we live.

I volunteered to bring some soft drinks down to the lakeside dock where we would gather for photos of our family happily fishing and boating and lounging together. (Conveniently absent from the pictures would be typical family squabbles, whining about the heat, and taking turns accidentally snagging one another in the shins with worm-baited fishhooks.)

As I sauntered down the pier with a tray full of refreshments, the jokes commenced.

"Hey Mom!" Gabe hollered in my direction. "Are you sure you can handle serving Dr. Pepper without Jane's help?"

"Yeah," chimed in Jim the photographer, relaxed and feeling almost part of the family at this point. "I hope you can handle pouring drinks into cups without the aid of a professional food stylist and all."

"Very funny," I chirped as I sat the tray down on a table.

I picked up a two-liter bottle of Dr. Pepper and heard an ominous fizzing sound near the cap. "Ooops," I said, "it sounds like it might have gotten shook up as I walked down the pier. I'd better open it over the LAAAaaaa . . . ."

At which point everything in my world went dark and wet.

When I surfaced above water, gasping for breath, I saw six startled faces staring into the lake where I found myself floating next to a large bobbing bottle of Dr. Pepper. I could not believe it. All I had had to do was open a soft drink bottle and pour a few drinks. A task even the most inexperienced of homemakers (or kindergarteners) should be able to handle. Now I suddenly found myself—boots, jeans, dignity, and Dr. Pepper—swimming in the lake.

"Is she all right?" I heard Jim ask my husband, Scott.

Scott's response was remarkably laid-back, having grown accustomed to my mishaps after twenty-five years. "Oh, yeah," he nodded in my gurgling, gagging, arm-waving direction. "She does this kind of stuff all the time. Go ahead and take some pictures of her before we fish her out. It'll make a great story."

And so, perhaps you can now understand why it is with no small sense of trepidation that I mentally gear up to tackle a regulation-sized turkey this Thanksgiving day.

To help prepare myself for the big moment, I'm reading the *Joy of Cooking* alongside *Feel the Fear and Do It Anyway*.

My grandmother and my mother before me were wonderful cooks and amazing hostesses. I cannot blame my cooking disorder on faulty upbringing or lack of training.

One skill, however, that my mother taught me early on stays with me and continues as a female family tradition: she taught me that part of being a truly beautiful woman is learning to enjoy a good laugh at yourself. (She also taught me to write down the embarrassing or unusual things I do quickly, then retell them or write them in journals. Ultimately she helped launch a career where I now make an actual profit from talking and writing about all the messes I get myself into. We may have a few dysfunctions in our family, but at least we have the decency to make them sound entertaining.)

Every year, as "we gather together to ask the Lord's blessing," my husband asks each one of us to share something we are thankful for. This year my kids may very well say something like, "We are thankful the turkey isn't made from tofu this year." Or, "We are grateful for fire extinguishers in every room." My husband may say he is thankful for take-out food and good restaurants.

But I will be thankful for a mother who—though she wasn't able to teach me to be a great cook—taught me the incredible, redemptive power of a good belly laugh.

So if your Thanksgiving meal doesn't exactly look like a photo spread for *Better Homes and Gardens*, if the day leaves you exhausted, or riddled with too many relatives in small quarters for too many hours, remember that if at some point you have prayed with gratitude in your heart to the Maker of humans and turkeys (or human turkeys), and you have laughed out loud with one or two others, you will have experienced a truly blessed Thanksgiving.

"Then our mouth was filled with laughter. . . . The Lord has done great things for us; whereof we are glad" (Psalm 126:2 KJV).

As you can see, I adopted my mother's writing skills, and her ability to create a home much like *I Love Lucy*'s in terms of slapstick humor, but I never quite got the hang of homemaking. Still I managed to make a part-time living as a caterer for three years and even cleaned houses for other people. (If I get paid for cooking and cleaning and see it as a "job," I do surprisingly well. But somehow, I can't seem to talk my husband and kids into giving me money for cooking a casserole.)

So, to whom would I turn for help with this chapter other than the woman who raised homemaking and hospitality to a fine art? None other than my mother, Ruthie Arnold, who was also coauthor of my first two books. I asked her to write her best hints on how to help her young daughter find her way around the kitchen—especially if she herself is no Galloping Gourmet.

Mom's Home Cooking by Ruthie Arnold

Cook!? Cook, you say? I don't even have time to cook myself, much less teach my daughter to cook!

What about talking with other moms—in your neighborhood, your church, maybe at your child's school—and finding out who Susie Homemaker is among you. Then, ask her to conduct some basic cooking classes in her home for all your young daughters. I can almost guarantee that if Susie approaches this with good humor and a sense of fun, the girls will love it.

Just think—your daughter discovers that once she learns to brown hamburger or ground turkey in a skillet with chopped onions, garlic powder, salt, and a dash of pepper, she can go from there to Italian, Mexican, or Southwest cuisine in minutes, depending on the spices she adds. Countless dishes rise triumphantly from just such a skillet, including those made from the addition of boxed mixes or canned pastas, soups, and beans.

Once the girls learn to boil pasta—not too long, but just right—the possibilities are truly endless.

Easy wonders can also be achieved by teaching our girls to wrap meat, fish, or fowl tightly in foil, season, and bake in an oven for the proper length of time for the particular food she chooses. Add peeled potatoes, carrots, or onions and—voila!—complete meals.

If you can just teach your daughter how to cook dried beans, you have taught her the best secrets of good tasting, nutritious, inexpensive, one-dish meals. (A crockpot is perfect for this—with an onion and a piece of bacon or ham tossed in. Otherwise, beans tend to boil over and burn.) It may be that someday in the future while she and her Prince Charming are finishing their educations, this may be survival food. In Texas, we love refried beans—simply put a cupful of pintos and their juices in a blender and reheat in a skillet. Wonderful on warmed soft corn or flour tortillas or atop crisp tortilla chips for nachos. And with the variety of beans, once again, the possibilities are almost endless.

Let's not forget the eggs. Scrambled, fried—the basics that will make a lot of quick suppers even if there are no breakfast eaters in the house, heaven forbid! My grandson, Zeke, loved to create omelets for his after-school snacks—tossing in chopped veggies, leftover meat, and cheese. Zeke enjoyed experimenting in the kitchen so much that I bought him a chef's hat. One thing about my daughter Becky professing to not be the world's greatest cook is that her kids were highly motivated to learn their way around a kitchen for sheer survival!

Once your daughter knows how to make toast, she will have discovered the Eighth Wonder of the World. She can go from simple toast to cinnamon toast for breakfast, cheese toast for lunch, bread sprinkled with seasoned salt before toasting—and serve this for dinner in a nice bread basket, even to company.

Fit in lessons on preparing vegetables and learning to love them. These jewels are virtually medicinal in their powers, and as we all know by now, probably the most neglected of all foods in the American diet. Let's face it. If we're going to have long life and good days, somebody's gonna have to peel, dice, and chop! And it may be that your daughter is the one who will help you take up the chopping knife and get veggies on the table.

The most simple salads can be sliced green peppers, celery, and carrot sticks, easy to have prepared before meals, and can often balance a main dish nicely. One way to get the kids to eat their veggies is to set a plate of these goodies out on the counter while you're preparing supper, and they're starving. Be sure to act like you'd rather they wait to eat them. Another quick and easy salad is sliced tomatoes, topped with a few onion rings for those who like them. Becky tells me that her daughter, Rachel, is the best fresh salad maker in the family. With a good variety of dressings, and some interesting additions to the fresh veggies—croutons, bacon bits, raisins or Craisins, pine nuts or candied walnuts, and a sprinkling of cheddar, feta, or goat cheese—salads can make wonderful meals.

Baked potatoes! Show your daughter how to microwave or bake potatoes, and demonstrate the endless variety of toppings for a quick treat—my kids use everything from barbecue sauce to Ranch dressing to taco meat or cheese and broccoli soup for potato toppers. A quick healthy treat is to slice up a potato into rounds, sprinkle with seasoned salt, and bake them on a cookie sheet, slightly greased with olive oil. You can also do this in the microwave with a plate inverted on top of another plate.

And don't forget the sweet potatoes. Served plain with butter, they dress up a meal, and with a little brown sugar and a marshmallow, they can serve as dessert. Good for the kids, but they'll never suspect.

Desserts? They seem to fall from the sky in this country, so let's not waste too much time teaching the girls how to make them, other than maybe one lesson in cake mixes, instant puddings, and sliced refrigerator cookies from the grocery store. If your daughter is going to learn dessert making, start with a cookbook of more healthful desserts and help to avoid the diabetes epidemic. One of my regrets as a mother of the '60s and '70s is the amount of emphasis I put on making wonderful tasting, but sugar-loaded desserts. I paid the price for these sugar years in my health down the road and had to relearn how to enjoy the simple, natural sweetness of fruits and whole grains with just a little bit of sweetening. If I could do it again, I would have cooked and served mostly healthy goodies for my children, with only the occasional splurge of a birthday cake or holiday dessert.

Just for Fun

Give your daughter lots of experience in smart shopping. Have her plan a week's worth of meals and make out the grocery list, keeping under a set budget. She can even do the shopping while you sit in the grocery café and read a book and enjoy a cup of coffee. Her reward? If she uses coupons to save money—allow her to keep the money saved and you both win big!

Generally, kids love dried fruit and nuts mixed with any kind of cereal or toasted oats, and Becky tells me that this is really the way her family most often satisfies their sweet tooth in a hurry.

Remember the Sewing Machine?

Although I do not sew anymore, one of my favorite memories as a girl of nine or ten was my mother teaching me and my best friend, Allison, how to sew. First a jumper, then some doll clothes, and gradually, I was shopping for material and patterns as a teenager, spending many a happy hour at the humming machine as an old Saturday night rerun or movie played in the background. I can also do embroidery, crochet, and crewel—and though I now fill most of my free time with carpooling, writing, traveling, and correspondence, one day I suspect I will take up needle and thread again, because it was such a relaxing, fun activity. Once again, I asked my mother, the homemaking expert, how she did it!

Tips from a Sewin' Granny by Ruthie Arnold

Moms may find they do themselves a favor when they sneak up on their daughters and start sewing lessons early. There are kits available for early grade school girls that teach the wonderful skill of pushing a needle in and out of a piece of paper or cardboard to form a picture. Small looms are available to be used with purchased loops to make pot holders. These can keep a little girl happily occupied all the way through a rainy afternoon and give her a taste of the creative art that sewing is.

If you really want to delight a young girl's heart, find a small doll, locate a good supply of fabric pieces and safe scissors, and show her how to cut holes in the fabric for the head and arms for her doll. From there she can go to colored shoe strings for belts, fabric glue for glitter, and sequins and other trims.

By the age of eight, a girl can learn to embroider, and what a delight this is. Of course, if Mom has never learned, it may be time for the Susie Seamstress Club to convene, formed on the order of the Susie Homemaker Club mentioned above. Failing this, look for the nearest traditional grandmother you can find, and save this vanishing skill.

By the age of ten, a girl can begin to learn to operate a sewing machine, a skill that is enormously helpful throughout life. It may not be used for more than sewing a ripped seam or patching a torn garment, but probably the most helpful sewing ability a girl can have is to learn to shorten a pair of pants. It may not be forever fashionable to have your pants legs bunched around your ankles.

A girl at the age of twelve can certainly begin to learn to sew simple garments, and some may take off like a rocket and become virtual dress designers. Some will acquire (and later appreciate) just the basics. I still laugh about Becky's sister, Rachel, and her brief sewing career. At about age twelve, she went through the hoops and very capably produced a wearable blouse. I was ecstatic—until Rachel thanked me very much, closed the machine, and never returned to it. (A word of explanation: Not only is Becky's sister, my younger daughter, named Rachel, but Becky named her own daughter Rachel after her sister. Rachel, Becky's sister, also married a man named Scott, as did Becky. Then Scott's brother married a girl named Becky. Family gatherings are interesting to say the least, with two people answering to almost every name.)

I, on the other hand, having sewed from the age of twelve, produced many of my daughters' clothes through high school, and Rachel, having learned what was involved, was enormously appreciative. Away at college, she called home and asked me if I would make her first formal for a college event, rather than buy one.

I turned out a red satin strapless gown, sequined and completed by a red velvet jacket, a designer dress made just to complement Rachel's dark skin and long dark curls. And, to my delight, when it was time for Rachel's wedding, she wanted her dress to be homemade—and made exactly like the wedding dress I had made for myself thirty years before. Not a problem, nor were the flower girl's dress, the two ring bearers' suits, and some of the bridesmaids' dresses (as well as many of Becky's bridesmaids' dresses with cascades of eyelet ruffles flowing down the back).

Somewhere along the way, your daughter may be up for learning to knit, crochet, or to discover the delight to be found in needlepoint and crewel works of art. Hooking rugs can be a wonderful way for a girl to pass the long afternoons of summer before high school and she becomes too busy. But if she learns these skills while she is young, they will be there for her when she may want them as an adult and doesn't have time for lessons. She will thank you for encouraging her and providing for them in her past.

Housekeeping Fun

Thank you so much, Mother, for your terrific input, and for giving me skills I can call upon when I really need them and mostly for the wonderful mother-daughter memories.

How can I make housekeeping sound like delightful fun for you and your daughter? I can only hope she is not as innovative as I was at avoiding these lessons. How did I know by instinct just when my mother's patience had reached the breaking point in regard to the state of my room? I don't know, but I always managed to hop in bed, prop myself up on pillows, and have my open Bible before me when she threw my bedroom door open. Usually, she would quietly turn and tiptoe away.

Consequently, at our house, when anyone was looking for something they had lost, Mother always asked, "Have you looked under Becky's bed?" Some of the time we were even able to laugh about it together, and cherish a column written by Erma Bombeck years ago when she was trying to clean her daughter's room. Suddenly, Erma turned to see a giant black spider crouching on her daughter's desk. She grabbed a shoe and pounded it almost into the desktop before she realized it was a dried banana peel.

Needless to say, housekeeping is not my forte, and I have written book after book on my failings in that area. Even though I have enjoyed the success of the books I've written about the state of my present housekeeping, it is true that it complicates my life enormously. It is always a challenge to find anything, including the cordless phone. I once had to run down the road to my friend Melissa's house and ask her to call me on the phone when I got back home. This way, I could hear my phone ringing and find it. It turned out to be in my unmade bed.

Having said all that, this is my suggestion for teaching girls the essential art of house cleaning: Find an enterprising woman who cleans houses for a living and ask her to hire your daughter as an assistant for a few weeks. If necessary, pay her for taking your daughter on. Seriously.

In the meantime, however, I have corralled some of my best housekeeping survival tools. Feel free to pass them on to your daughter, especially if she turns out to be one of us creative, artsy sorts who finds comfort in a little bit of clutter, and needs extra help focusing. If you happened to have a daughter who is a neat freak, you don't need this chapter anyway!

- **The Clean Sweep.** Help your daughter get in the habit of getting everything up and out of sight before dinnertime or bedtime. If she has a wooden floor, she can literally sweep a pile into a closet with a huge broom or rake and shut the door. She may have to lean on it really hard. Now, yes, the pile is still there—behind the door—to be reckoned with, but perhaps you can have her do this on a long afternoon on Saturday or Sunday and just be satisfied with the clutter out of your eyesight until this happens.

- **Sing a Song.** On my Cheerful Mother Days, I'd enlist the kids' help by singing the tidying-up song ("A Spoon Full of Sugar") from Mary Poppins in my best English Nanny soprano. I also managed a pretty good dwarf imitation with a rousing rendition of "Hi-Ho-Hi-Ho, To Clean Our Room We Go!" The kids loved it until they hit about age seven, when my singing suddenly embarrassed them. So, at that point I began using my singing as a threat: "If you don't clean your room, I'm gonna start with the SHOWTUNES!" This was guaranteed to send them scrambling for a broom and dustpan.

- **Organize One Drawer or Shelf Per Day.** Pick a short, five-minute task to help you and your daughter feel in control of *something* again. For me, a right-brained messy person, it is way too daunting to think of cleaning and organizing a whole room! So I've found that breaking jobs up into short tasks really helps. Often it is like popcorn. After I organize one drawer, I think, *Hey, that wasn't too bad,* and I may even go for cleaning out two or three of them!

- **Share the Chores and Rotate.** When I was teaching school, I had to have a lot of help from my children to keep up with the house, so we rotated room monitoring duties. One week Rachel was responsible for the kitchen; Gabe for the living room; Zach for the car; Zeke for the bathrooms, and so on. They were not responsible to clean *everything* up themselves but they were responsible to delegate and make sure things stayed picked up in their designated room. We switched rooms and responsibilities the following week.

- **Yelp for Help!** As a grown woman with a home-based career, I can now hire a housekeeper to come in once a week. But if your daughter isn't the Queen of Clean, she probably can't afford to hire someone to come clean her bedroom on her babysitting salary. Suggest that she have a good friend come over one afternoon after school or on a Saturday and have a room cleaning/organizing party. Let them turn up the music, serve them snacks between cleaning, and let them go for it. Then your daughter can go to her friend's house and help *her* get organized. Messies like company and stay motivated on a task as long as there is some fun and sociability involved.

- **Use Open Baskets and Boxes Without Lids for Organizing Her Room.** Girls tend to use open containers that they can toss papers, clothes, or shoes into without effort more than drawers or shelves. Hooks are easier to use than hangers so make these abundant in your daughter's room and closet.

- **Reward At Regular Intervals.** Teach your daughter to play a mental game with herself: if she cleans her closet, she can go take a hot bubble bath. When she hangs up all her clothes, she can lay down on the bed and listen to her favorite CD. She can talk on the phone while she organizes a drawer.

- **Buy a Cute Timer for Her Room.** Messies work well under pressure and thrive with applause. Have her set the timer for five minutes, see how much she can get done in that time, and come applaud her for her amazing five-minute feats.

- **Buy Something New for Her Room.** This is a trick I've often played on myself. I buy a new throw pillow for the couch, and wanting to see the stunning effect of the pillow, I suddenly realize I have to first move the laundry off of the couch in order to *see* the pillow at all. This leads to wild activities like vacuuming, dusting, and straightening up—all so I could appreciate the beauty of the new pillow on the couch in all its glory. Fresh flowers can have the same effect on me. Who can appreciate a vase of fresh daisies on a kitchen counter piled up with last night's dishes? Company coming is always a great motivator.

Rave Review

A terrific little resource for teaching organization to your daughter is a booklet for helping to organize your children at their various ages and stages. It can be ordered from Marcia Ramsland on her website at www.organizingpro.com. Click "children's booklet" and check out the resources for you too, Mom! Have an organizing question for Marcia? Write her at Marcia@organizingpro.com.

Her Dream Room

One of the activities I most loved, from as far back as I can remember, was creating and decorating tiny rooms for my miniature dolls. Given a shoe box, scissors, fabric scraps, paper muffin liners, spools of thread, ribbon, almost any tiny item, tape, and glue, I could be content for a week. One day I'd make my tiny dolls a bedroom, the next it might be a living room with spool chairs and a bar soap coffee table with a couch made from a washrag, folded and pinned just so—then I'd tape the boxes together to create one big maze of a house.

Even a child who leans toward disorganization might find her homemaking wings in decorating—for here is where all her creative talents come in to play. You may have a budding interior decorator under your roof. One of the most fun decorating projects a mother and daughter can enjoy is to create your daughter's dream bedroom.

To get the decorating juices flowing, pick up copies of magazines with decorating ideas in them: *Better Homes and Gardens, Country Living,* or *Victoria* are fun places to start. (Also see the decorating books on page 156.) Let your daughter cut up pictures and "decorate" a fantasy room on a piece of construction paper. Furniture or department store advertising slicks (found in most Sunday newspapers) or catalogs can be fun to look at and cut up too!

If you are on a budget, all the better because you will have to get very creative and shop for the best bargains. Most girls love a challenge. In fact, I gave my daughter Rachel a $150 budget one Christmas for the sole purpose of decorating her room. This had to cover everything: bedspread, furniture, paint, accessories, and curtains. She chose hot pink and silver for her colors and away she went: First to the paint store for a gallon of Pink Panther paint, and a quart of light pink to accent the trim. She and her father disappeared for a day into her attic bedroom, and emerged covered in pink, but proud of the transformation that a coat of paint can bring to any room. Next they hauled her black metal headboard into the backyard and spray painted it silver, in addition to all the trim on her white furniture, plus several other accessories. We found the perfect fluffy pink, white, and silver comforter and pillows, lamps, and curtains at Target—on sale! Within a couple of weeks, she was sitting pretty in pink.

I had a sunshine yellow bedroom all of my teen years, and though I'd change the style (mod '70s to country chic)—I stayed with yellow because the color always brightened and cheered me, even during the worst teen angst. Remind your daughter, before she begins picking out colors, that colors will affect her mood. Here's the most common colors and the effects they have on us:

- **Yellow:** happy
- **Pink:** feminine
- **Soft Blue:** calm and cool
- **Purple:** fun
- **Soft whites, creams, tans:** relaxing, uncluttered
- **Orange:** artsy, fun
- **Red:** warm
- **Green:** refreshing

Television and Book Mentors

Since childhood, I have always loved watching homemaking, craft, gardening, and cooking shows and find that even a not-so-great-homemaker like me can feel suddenly inspired as I watch shows like *Martha Stewart Living* or *Rebecca's Garden*. Books by Tasha Tudor or Alexandria Stoddard inspire the hidden homemaker in me with their enthusiastic and simple strategies for creating beauty in every corner of their lives. Just reading through pretty decorating and idea books or magazines, even without following a single suggestion, is soothing and inspirational to me—and a moment easily shared over a cup of hot cocoa or tea with your daughter.

The Hidden Art of Homemaking and *What Is a Family?* are timeless classics by Edith Schaeffer that remind us of what matters most in our homes, and how to make memories of otherwise mundane moments. Though these books are over two decades old now, they are still in print, and I was delighted to discover how many young women are discovering Edith's inspirational writing and taking her advice to heart as I browsed the recent reviews.

Rave Reviews

Here are some fun decorating books to get your started. Look in your local library for books, and bring home an armload of ideas for the two of you to browse through.

The Big Book of Kids' Rooms: Everything You Need to Create the Perfect Room for Your Child (Leisure Arts, 2000)

Decorating for Good: A Step-By-Step Guide to Rearranging What You Already Own by Carole Talbott and Maggie Matthews (Clarkson Potter, 1999)

Decorating Kids' Rooms: Nurseries to Teen Retreats by Linda Hallam and Sharon L. Novotne O'Keefe (Meredith Books, 1997)

The Smart Approach to Kids' Rooms: Planning, Designing, Decorating by Megan Connelly and Kathie Robitz (Creative Homeowner Press, 2000)

Use What You Have Decorating: Transform Your Home in One Hour with Ten Simple Design Principles by Lauri Ward (Perigee, 1999)

Living on a Budget

Ellie Kay, mother of five and author of *Money Doesn't Grow On Trees: Teaching Your Kids the Value of a Buck*, writes, "Teaching kids about budgeting, saving, tithing, and investing is what the real world is all about. They won't graduate from high school and start making $50,000 a year as a vice president with an expense account—they'll have to earn both over many years. Preparing our children means being transparent about our finances and showing them what we really do with our money. This will give them life skills that will give them a real advantage in real life."

One of the best things you can do with your daughter is talk about how your family income is used to pay bills. Show her *your* budgeting system, with the reminder of course that she is not to share how much your family income actually is.

Here's a way we give our kids a "taste" of budgeting their own money. Rather than telling our children they can have so many pairs of pants or shirts or shoes for school shopping, we give them a budget to shop with. They are incredibly motivated to find the best bargains, knowing their wardrobe has to last, at least until Christmas.

Ellie also tells her children, "Just because you are alive doesn't mean you get an allowance," emphasizing the importance of tying in financial compensation with actual work done-for-hire. On her website at www.elliekay.com, Ellie gives a whole slew of ideas and ways for kids to earn money—along with some great tips for moms as well.

While you are Internet browsing, also check out www.biggerbetterbargains.com for all sorts of ways to save money on everything you can think of! I listen to "the shopping diva"—who runs the website—on a local Dallas station and she is not only fun to listen to, she can help you find just about anything you need at a bargain price. You can even email her your questions!

God, Mom, and Me

Proverbs 15:17—"Better a meal of vegetables where there is love than a fattened calf with hatred."

Proverbs 17:1—"Better a dry crust with peace and quiet than a house full of feasting, with strife."

If you have a concordance, look up the word *hospitable* and the verses that go with this concept. To be hospitable comes from the thought of "loving strangers"—making people feel a part of your home and family.

What are some practical ways you can make people feel welcome in your home?

Most of us love a clean house, great homemade meals, and nice decorating. But as much as we enjoy these (when we can have them!), they are not the things that matter most in a home.

Ask your daughter, "Would you rather have a hot dog on a paper plate in a friend's house where everyone is glad you came, or the best steak dinner served on gorgeous china plates—where everyone was in a bad mood and arguing?"

Encourage, by example, a relaxed homemaking style that allows for a few messes and impromptu conversations. When it comes to cooking and decorating—remember simple is always in style. Ultimately, your daughter will remember your love and a relaxed atmosphere much more than a clean kitchen floor or designer furniture.

Sugar 'n' Spice in the Family Tree

Helping Your Daughter Enjoy Her Legacy

I received a call from my publisher in Nashville asking me to come speak at their sales conference. I thought this would be the perfect opportunity for a little mother-daughter getaway.

Rachel looked dubious. "Mom, are you sure you can get both of us to the airport and get a rental car and follow a map and all?"

"Yes, Rachel," I responded, a little hurt by her lack of confidence in her ol' mom. "And this may come as a shock, but I can also comb my own hair and tie my shoes too."

We landed in Nashville without a hitch and in this city, rich in history, Rachel opted to spend the day at the Great American Outlet Mall. We must have spent five hours shopping that day, missing nary a nook, cubby, or cranny. We had an absolute ball at that mall.

That is, until the sun went down and the air grew nippy, our stomachs began growling and our feet begged for relief—and

I realized I'd lost the key to the rental car. An hour and a half after retracing our every step—up nooks, around cubbies, and down crannies—we finally found the precious keys in the corner of a remote dressing room.

"Mom," Rachel said, her voice trembling from cold and fatigue as we walked to the car, "you are going to give me gray hair before I'm fourteen."

In an effort to cheer her I purchased a pizza, two coloring books, and a box of crayons on the way to the hotel. That night we sat in our fluffy robes on our respective beds, watching *Touched by an Angel* and a charming movie called *A Thousand Men and a Baby*. I glanced over at Rachel's side of the room, and couldn't help noting that her clothes were folded as neatly as little party sandwiches. Even her toiletries were aligned in ascending order.

"Rach," I said, "your side of the room looks like its been touched by an angel."

She glanced over at the pile of clothes on my bed and replied, "Mom, looks like a thousand men and a baby had a party on your side of the room."

We went on to have a fun time together, and then, before we knew it, it was time to return to Texas. While we were standing at the ticket counter in the Nashville airport I looked down and noticed my suitcase had just exploded! The zipper had popped off and my clothes were poofing from the seams around my feet. (If you want to mortify a teenage girl, stand next to her in an airport with your underwear lying on the floor around you.)

I ended up having to patch up the suitcase with a roll of duct tape the ticket agent handed to me. (You know you're a redneck if you latch your Samsonite with duct tape . . .) Rachel disappeared at this point.

Finally I found her; we flew home to Dallas, retrieved our

luggage—both latched and duct-taped—and began searching for my car in the parking lot.

This turned out to be more difficult than planned, and after about thirty minutes of huffing and puffing up aisles of parked cars I went into survival mode.

"Rachel, you sit here with the suitcases," I ordered. "I'll run up and down and look for our car."

On one return trip I noticed Rachel munching on a cookie as she sat morosely staring into space atop our pile of luggage.

"Where'd you get that?" I asked.

"A lady came by and said, 'Hon, you look like you could use a cookie.'" With fire in her eyes, Rachel continued, "Mom! She thought I was *homeless!*"

Eventually we found the car. We were so happy to be headed home after our long ordeal. When both of us were belted into the front seats, I turned the key in the ignition.

Nothing.

"Oops," I said quietly. "Guess I left the lights on all weekend. The battery appears to be dead."

At this point Rachel's chin begin to quiver and I had to get tough.

"Hey, Rach! Buck up! We're Thelma and Louise, remember? Why, we are a pair of brave women, like Helen Keller and Anne Sullivan!"

"Mom," she said flatly, all expression gone from her eyes. "Give it up. We're Dumb and Dumber."

There's nothing more fun than girls-only get-away trips, as long as you accept that something will probably go wrong along the way. However, even the worst experiences will usually make the funniest stories when you get back home. I've told the above story dozens of times and it never fails to make us laugh. I remember reading somewhere that our children usually don't remember the high points of family trips as much as they remember the crazy, unexpected episodes. Most of the stories that follow the introduction "Remember the time when ..." end up being stories of being caught off-guard, or a bizarre series of events, or a really bad day that turned out to be humorous.

So don't worry if your special family trips and carefully planned events have a few hitches. Sometimes it's the hitches that keep us in stitches.

Here are some hints for keeping your relationship with your daughter and the family running smoothly—even when life throws you a curve.

You Gotta Keep Talkin'

Have you heard the one about the five-hundred-pound canary? When he sings, you listen!

Good communication is the bedrock of any relationship, and the bedrock of good communication is good listening. This is true in all our relationships, but I think it is especially true with our teen and preteen daughters. So when they are ready to talk, we will be wise if we make sure we're listening. Postponing the talk can mean it never happens, at least not on the particular topic they had in mind that day. On rare occasions, that can come back to haunt us.

Here are some communication tips to remember and use.

- When we really listen to our daughters, we are showing them respect, which should in turn produce respect in them for us and for our opinions and wishes. We can encourage our husbands to put down the book or newspaper, or turn off the TV when their daughters are available for conversation.
- Rather than making dogmatic statements to our girls, try asking questions such as, "Do you think you're handling this in the best way?" "Have you thought that such and such may happen?" "Have you consid-

ered how your friend may be feeling?" There are two questions we can ask that often open doors to us in their minds and hearts. They are, "What do you think about . . . ?" and "How do you feel about . . . ?"

- We need to be cautious about our responses to our daughters' statements, and again treat them with respect.
- We can take advantage of impromptu moments, and also plan time alone with her, or encourage time alone with her dad, particularly in settings she will enjoy and where she will feel at ease. A trip to the ice cream parlor with Dad, or a shopping morning and lunch with Mom, are times when we may have opportunities to know what is going on in their lives and minds that we might otherwise miss.

If we can build good communication and intimacy with our daughters before they become teenagers, it should make the teen years easier.[5]

Staying Close

We have all heard the maxim "The family that prays together, stays together." It might also be said, "The family that plays together, stays together." Certainly, they will have a lot of fun! In fact, the most well-adjusted adults who carry on with the faith of their childhood were, for the most part, raised in homes where their parents could enjoy a deep, spiritual conversation over coffee one minute, and be falling on the floor with laughter the next.

---

[5]Thank you, once again, to my own mom, who helped me compile the above list, and was—and still is—the world's best listener. It may be the thing I love most about her, perhaps because it is so rare. I can only name a handful of people who consistently give the gift of rapt attention to others, and my mother heads that list!

I asked my mother about this recently and she agreed. "Becky, so many adults live with regrets that the years they were raising their children flew by and were over, almost before they knew it. They never did the things with their kids that could have made their family so much happier, and given them so many more happy memories to carry with them as they left home. Some even regret the many hours they spent in church services and activities without achieving a balance in playing together. I also wonder if some families don't regret the number of organized activities their children were involved in, if there was no time left just for being together in a relaxed way."

A poignant truth.

For children *do* love playing and having a good time with their families. And having a lot of those kinds of experiences takes some time and planning and commitment. It especially takes cultivating a fun-loving attitude in our own hearts, a willingness to let our dignity go, and to learn to find delight in our children.

Though there are many times when something you love to do happens to fit with something your daughter likes (shopping, sewing, playing cards), there are many times when you'll have to put your own desires on the back burner in order to meet your daughter's need for fun and play. (Cutting out paper dolls, coloring a picture, reading a book for the twentieth time . . .) What does your daughter really like to do? If at all possible, make an effort to join her in that activity. We're not talking the need for big money here, either.

"A watermelon feast in the backyard on a summer's evening, climaxed by quiet conversation, or even a few songs, can be the stuff of which memories are made," my mother reminisced. "In the wintertime, marshmallows roasted in the fireplace and a story or two can be a gift to any family."

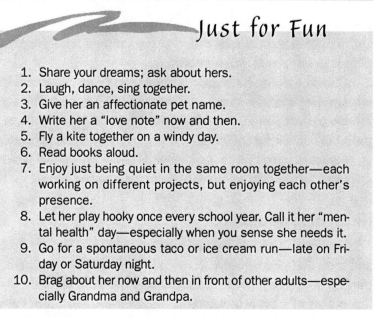

Just for Fun

1. Share your dreams; ask about hers.
2. Laugh, dance, sing together.
3. Give her an affectionate pet name.
4. Write her a "love note" now and then.
5. Fly a kite together on a windy day.
6. Read books aloud.
7. Enjoy just being quiet in the same room together—each working on different projects, but enjoying each other's presence.
8. Let her play hooky once every school year. Call it her "mental health" day—especially when you sense she needs it.
9. Go for a spontaneous taco or ice cream run—late on Friday or Saturday night.
10. Brag about her now and then in front of other adults—especially Grandma and Grandpa.

Family Photo Albums

Creating a family photo album is a great way to help your daughter appreciate her legacy. Keeping a family album and scrapbook can help your daughter see how special a family is, and to know that she is an important part of that family. Also, it can be a lot of fun for a daughter to keep up the family scrapbook/album. You may have to get the ball rolling by assembling the scrapbook, scotch tape, fine-tip black marker, and the pictures together for your young secretary. Wallpaper books with tiny prints make great "backgrounds" for pictures. Stickers are also lots of fun.

Go through your photos with your daughter, assemble them according to approximate dates or periods in the life of the family, discard poor or duplicate snapshots, and create a page or two as examples. You are now ready to start the scrapbook together! Our family always enjoyed using cutouts from greeting cards or magazines to add humor around the pictures, and maybe a sentence or two written below identifying the people in the photo when necessary.

Once the album has a good beginning and your daughter sees what we are about, we need to relax and not be picky. The aim is not a perfect album, it is a functioning one that will make her proud of being a part of a fun and loving family. It has become a great relief to bring home a new batch of pictures from the developer and turn it over to my daughter to put in the album.

Girls-Only Getaway

Last year my sister, Rachel, moved to Texas from the East, and soon declared we were having a Girls-Only Getaway at our parents' retirement home in the quaint little town of Granbury, Texas. Part of what motivated her was that she had a new baby daughter to show off, after a prolonged drought of baby girls in the family. In fact, the last girl baby born to our family was eighteen years ago—my daughter, Rachel.

Even with baby Tori and her cousin Rachel, we still don't have many girls to draw from for a reunion. With my dad's sister, Aunt Ann, there were just six of us, but we had a wonderful time, prowling the town square, seeing the variety show, lunch at the tea room. Since then, we have added another girl—our Zeke's wife, Amy. I hope this is the first getaway of many, and that as Tori grows up, she will have a delicious sense that she is a cherished member of our sisterhood, and feel very special because of it.

My friend and personal assistant, Rose Dodson, was immediately adopted into a family of many women when she married her husband, Fred, whose mother had six sisters! Rose's mother-in-law purchased a time-share option, and every year all the families they can pick from the family tree head off on a road trip to a luxury condo in a different location.

Another wonderful grandmother, Mary Sue, who lives in our neck of the woods, had her retirement house built with her large family in mind. There is even a slide going down from the second story of their home. Because Mary Sue is a homemaker extraordinaire and loves having family around her, she opens her home—all summer long—for her kids and grandkids to stay and play, as long as they like. Often her daughter and daughter-in-law will stay for a month at a time during the summer, as the cousins fish, swim, and water ski together. The men? Well, they come in on weekends between working all week. For a month, however, it's mostly womenfolk and kids. What a relaxed time of family bonding they have, and memories to last their children and grandchildren a lifetime.

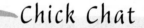

Chick Chat

Take some time to list every female you and your daughter can think of in your family tree. What quality does she most admire in each one? Perhaps there are some women or teens in the family who have made poor choices with their lives. What has your daughter learned *not* to do from observation? Talk about ways this relative might be able to turn her life around if she wanted to do so.

Larger Family Reunions

My parents were recently invited for a Christmas dinner at the home of friends who literally have no extended family on either side. I hope it is hard for you to imagine what it would be like to look forward to Christmas Day and know there will be no extended family—only you, your husband (or possibly just you), and your children.

If we have family, it is important to gather together at times and celebrate the fact that we do. If your family doesn't have reunions, what would be the chances that you could arrange one? As I said, unless your family is really dysfunctional and you feel your child would be distressed in such a gathering, she will reap many good things from such a gathering. (My mother and I once wrote a book together called *Adult Children of Fairly Functional Parents*, realizing none of our families are perfectly functioning. I once heard a woman from Georgia say, "In the south, at least we have the decency to make our dysfunctions sound entertaining.") The sense of belonging to a family and a caring community is important to us all, but especially to kids during their growing-up years.

Family reunions can range from large, elaborately planned, all-weekend festivities in rented hotels to one-day, covered-dish gatherings in a local park. You might put out a puzzle to work, or set out some cards and dominoes and maybe a game of Taboo or Scrabble for those who prefer to visit over a game. Horseshoes, a volleyball net, or croquet are also great fun for larger groups of cousins, aunts, and uncles to play if the weather is nice.

This June our family will gather down in the piney woods just for a day at my Uncle George and Aunt Maurine's country home. Lunch will be catered Texas barbecue, we'll all pitch in to pay for it, and there will probably be about forty eager eaters. No planned program, just "vistin'," as we say in east Texas. A simple but wonderful thing.

For my nine-year-old nephew, Trevor, Tori's big brother, this will be his first full-blown family reunion this summer, since the family on his father's side is small and lives in the West. But he's caught on to the fun an extended family can be, and he's only met the fifteen or so of us that make up his mother's side of the family. We all look forward to his reaction when he finds out there's thirty more of us out there! This is one of the reasons his family moved him and his new baby sister to Texas—to meet a whole raft of aunts, uncles, cousins, and second cousins.

Let's celebrate the family that we have, as often as we can. And if you don't have relatives by blood, seek out and adopt "family" of your own. There are lonely widows in many churches and nursing homes who would love to be an adopted "grandma" or "auntie." Scott and I have "adopted" a family whose father is temporarily incarcerated. To the little girls we are "Aunt Becky and Uncle Scott"—and we feel like big brother and sister to this single mother who is carrying such a big load.

Rave Reviews

Family-Friendly Entertainment

Feature Films for Families—Super resource for videos and information that support traditional and family values. See www.familytv.com or 1–800–Family–TV for a free catalog. One of our favorites is a beautifully done, heart-touching movie with gorgeous music called *Rigoletto*. You can be sure that anything coming from this company is not only safe for your children, but supportive of families.

Hallmark Movies are often beautifully done films to rent or purchase—and they nearly always leave you feeling inspired and closer to family. *Sarah, Plain and Tall* is a beautiful story for any family, but perhaps especially for step-families. *Ellen Foster* is also excellent.

Family Friendly Movie Reviews—A terrific resource can be found at www.familystyle.com. This website also provides the top links to other family friendly entertainment resources.

Sisters: Songs of Friendship, Joy and Encouragement for Women—This CD has a wonderful song called "These Are the Women We Come From." Listen to it with a few of your female relatives.

Writing Families

From my earliest remembrance, when one of us kids would say something cute or profound, my mother would say—"Just a minute. I need to write that down." And she did. She put all our cute quotes and quips and funny stories on slips of paper or napkins and then stuffed them in big brown envelopes with our names on them. We loved reading through these as children and I know it is one of the reasons that my sister and I both write humor.

In his excellent book, *Families Writing*, Peter Stillman says,

> I don't know of a greater, wiser gift than words written down. Years back when my children were small, I somehow sensed the need to give them words of mine. In retrospect, it's clear that I was seeking ways to keep them and me together beyond the fleeting span of time between early childhood and their pushing off into the wider world, into lives mostly separate from mine. I expressed this need in a homely enough way: a series of sketches, each labeled "When I Was Your Age" and captioned with a sentence or two about what it was like to be seven or eight or twelve back when I was a kid.

What a great idea! Kids love notes from their parents, special letters or memories written down and delivered on special occasions or ordinary days, postcards when you are away from them—you can even write back and forth in a Mom and Me Journa, keeping a written running dialogue going. One mother told me that her daughter, who almost never talked but loved to write, found this to be a fabulous way to keep communication going.

Family Cookbooks

Blank journals, recipe cards in a special box, or photo album pages can be used to collect family recipes for your daughter.

One summer, as a preteen, I bought a recipe box and index cards with my allowance and set to work copying down my grandmother's, aunts', and mother's best recipes for "Someday When I Was Married." I still have and use those recipes written in my own twelve-year-old handwriting.

Family Newsletters (or Websites)

Let the kids help create a family newspaper and send it out to relatives in the summertime, rather than at Christmas when everyone's flooded with stuff to do and no time to read!

Family Christmas Cards

We have friends, Karl and Terri Kemp, who have each of their four children draw or write a page each Christmas. They photocopy the art or poem or essay and put it on card stock, sending out a five page "greeting" card that none of their friends can seem to throw away. I almost never keep cards, but every year I've kept the Kemp card—all of their friends and family look forward to it.

God, Mom, and Me

"God sets the lonely in families" (Psalm 68:6).

Talk to your daughter about people who don't have grandmas or grandpas, moms or dads, sisters or brothers. What are some ways your family might reach out to them and make them feel included and a part of a clan? Choose one thing you can do this week together to include someone in your family circle.

Read Galatians 5:22. Write out each "fruit" of the Spirit and talk about a relative in your family tree who exemplifies each fruit. Share about the fruit that you see in each other's life as well.

God Things

Leading Your Daughter to the Father

How many times has it been said that the world changed forever on September 11, 2001? That is no doubt true, and it is true physically (in terms of our freedom of movement), emotionally (in terms of feeling safe and secure), and spiritually, where the differences may be more profound than we realize. The question we moms face now is, "How do I comfort and console my daughters in their changed world?" How do I reassure them that God is their ultimate Comforter and Consoler, and that no matter what they may face in life, he will never leave them or forsake them?

A Comforting Shoulder

Certainly our world was not without its shocks, long before 9/11. You may already be having discussions with your daughter about her safety when she's in school. If not, I suggest we rely on the promise of 2 Corinthians 1:4: "We can comfort those in any trouble with the comfort we ourselves have received from God."

If we have not taught her to fly to the Rock that is Christ when she is afraid, now may be a wonderful time to begin. After all, isn't that where we fly?

I remember being very afraid as a girl of twelve or thirteen, particularly at the height of *The Late Great Planet Earth* phenomenon of the 1970s, the Vietnam War, and the dire predictions of what pollution, overpopulation, the energy crisis, and nuclear war would do to our planet. I often wondered if I'd live to graduate from high school in such a dangerous world. Would I ever fall in love? Get married? Have children?

One night I went to my mother's room, upset by the state of the world around me. Soothingly, she calmed and comforted my fears—by telling me about the times she was afraid and uncertain as a young girl too.

"Honey," she said, as she stroked my hair, "I was certain the world would come to an end when I was your age too. I grew up during Pear Harbor, on the heels of the Great Depression. And look at me! I've had a wonderful life—married a great guy, had three precious kids. Every generation has their own fears and troubles, but your future is bright, Becky. God will always be with you."

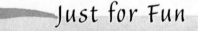

Just for Fun

The next time it rains, go outside together on the porch or up to the attic where you can really hear the rain splattering on the roof. Take mugs of hot chocolate and simply listen together. Or call your daughter outside, take her hand if she'll let you, to see a particularly beautiful sunset or cloud or bird or rainbow. It only takes a second or two—but you've made a memory moment she may cherish a lifetime. Talk about appreciating God's creation.

I find myself giving similar talks to my children and their friends, calming their fears with the very words my mother spoke to me, and I am sure my grandmother Nonnie spoke to her as a child. Our daughters deserve to look forward to their future!

Music to Calm the Worried Heart

There is a song on Michael W. Smith's Christmas album that always calms my fearful heart, and leaves it soaring every time I hear it. It's performed by a boy's choir and it simply says, first quietly, then crescendoing and ending in full chorus and orchestra, three wonderful words, "All is well." Like the old hymn "It is Well With My Soul," this song soothes my inner spirit. Find a song, hymn, or praise chorus on a well-loved CD that ministers quiet and peace to your heart. Keep it handy and play it for your daughter. Encourage her to find her own "peace song" to play when she needs to refocus her mind.

Prayer: A Place of Solace

Have we made it a practice to pray with our child when she has been either filled with joy and triumph or afraid and burdened? This doesn't mean we wait until we're all settled together in a perfect setting for family devotionals. It means we drop what we're doing during the course of her days, and as the opportunity arises, take her hand and pray with her then. Making the most of the moments of "felt need" are all important.

Our family has gathered in several huddles to hold each other through the years, as my husband, Scott, led us in prayers for the great needs of the moment. Twice we've lost young teenage boys in car accidents in our little town. The solid earth under our feet and our children's feet seems to shake at times like these, and for a time there is nothing to do but hold one another and pray and cry. And when the grieving subsides, we remind our children that this is not the end of a relationship, but only a short blip in the eternity we'll all spend together.

This summer, it was my daughter-in-law's much-loved eighteen-year-old brother, Justin, who was taken to heaven after a fatal car crash. For several months, and even now, it seems so unreal. My daughter, who had been friends with Justin most of her young life, drove to his graveside a day or two after the funeral, wanting to be alone to cry and grieve the loss of her friend, and her sister-in-law's beloved brother. I alerted Scott and he drove to the cemetery soon after, standing nearby, allowing his daughter the time she needed alone, but making sure she had someone to hold her as she exited.

The evening of 9/11, my husband came home early, gathered our children together, and prayed for our country and all who had lost loved ones. We didn't have to coerce our kids into going to church on the Sunday following this event. Like most of you reading this book, we wanted nothing more than to be with fellow believers, holding hands, singing, and praying: one nation, one family, under God. Perhaps it isn't until times like this that we really understand why the hassle of getting to and attending a church is so important. To whom else do we go when our heart is breaking but to God, and to the people who call on his name?

An Attitude of Gratitude

Equally important are prayers of thanksgiving and praise: for making the basketball team, for good grades, for a great day or a beautiful sunset—recognizing all good gifts fall from our Father's hand. In fact, one of my most blessed memories is my family, including my husband, Mom, Dad, midwife, and Zach and Zeke as little boys—surrounding my bedside as I held my newborn daughter, Rachel Praise, and giving God thanks for this precious new life, fresh from the womb.

I often compliment my kids on a job well done, and afterwards add how thankful I am that they have been wise with the gifts God has given them—a good mind, a kind heart, and a healthy body.

Quiet Time and Eden Spots

We can encourage our daughter, even at a young age, to have her own personal time alone with God each day. Have your own little "Eden Spot" where you go to spend time with God, and encourage your daughter to pick her own special nook as well. Some winter mornings I light a candle and grab my coffee, cuddling up with a quilt, and simply enjoy the communion between me and my Father. There are days I read Scripture, sometimes a devotional, and sometimes I just meditate on a verse memorized from childhood, and pray. And then I just soak up God's love, listening deep in my heart for his voice. It's all very natural, and nothing forced—moments of nurturing my spirit.

If you can see that your daughter loves to write, encourage her to write down her questions, doubts, and fears, and then pray specifically for answers, and for his peace to settle over her heart. The gift of a beautifully bound journal, or even a spiral notebook, can become a treasured friend to your daughter—a place where she can safely unburden all her pent-up thoughts. Perhaps you and she might take an afternoon to decorate a Quiet Time basket or tote bags in which to keep your journals, Bibles, devotionals, and a couple of good easy-flowing ink pens. (Make one a fun color to use for highlighting!) Be sure to respect her privacy where her journal or diary is concerned—unless she volunteers to share some entries with you, or is behaving in ways that seriously concern you (enough to risk losing her trust in order to possibly save her from danger).

There *are* numbers of daily devotional books available now for girls. You may want to choose one suited to your daughter's age and spiritual maturity to use during her devotional time. These can be rich with wisdom, comfort, encouragement, and challenges. Check out a few examples in the Rave Review section on page 183.

Bible Study

"A critical factor in her life will be how much of God's Word she stores away in her heart and mind," my mother, Ruthie, encouraged as we discussed this topic together. "Perhaps she can be encouraged to study her Sunday school quarterly as part of her devotional time, or perhaps in the evening before or after her homework is done. One of the most basic and helpful things we can do for our daughters is to teach them to recite the books of the Bible by heart. This might be included in homework time, or just for fun when riding in the car on trips, or on a rainy day when there's not much else to do. Once she knows these books in order, she can quickly find the passages she will be looking for—all her life."

I'm living proof that she's right! I still sing the little song she taught me when I'm looking for books of the New Testament, and it has saved me from fumbling for pages in church. (Now I have to admit, I once learned all the books of the Old Testament— Mother even made miniature books of the Bible out of matchboxes to help me. But I still get lost every time I have to look up a minor prophet. But then I am ye of little memory.)

Most church-based Wednesday night programs for girls, such as Pioneer Girls or Awanas, or Bible Memory Association Camps have systematic plans of memorizing Bible verses— great for kids who love order and predictability. However, if you have a creative child who loves to read, she might be more motivated to memorize verses that she picks out herself. I often helped my children memorize verses by creating a little tune out of them.

One caution: memorization can be a rote exercise with little meaning, unless we demonstrate how God's Word in our heart can help us through life's everyday pains.

When your daughter is fighting with her little brother, you might take her aside and say, "Honey, I know it's hard—especially when he gets on your last nerve. But remember the verse you memorized about being kind and tenderhearted and forgiving last week, the way Christ is tender and forgiving with us? Try to remember how patient God is with you as you deal with others." Or when she's afraid of giving a speech at school the next day, you might jot down a verse like, "God hasn't given us the spirit of fear, but of power and love and a sound mind," or, "At times I am afraid, I will trust in him," on an index card and tuck it in her lunch box or tape it to her bathroom mirror.

Youth Groups

Wouldn't it be wonderful if we could always assume that every adult and every activity in our child's lives would be wise and loving and have their best interests at heart? That whether it was a Sunday school class or a public school class, they would always be welcomed warmly, treated kindly, and be safe from damaging experiences?

Sadly, that is less and less a given in our world, and so it falls our lot as parents to know the adults who influence our children's lives or have responsibility for their supervision and safety. Good ones deserve all our applause and support. If you have serious questions or doubts, check it out!

In a perfect world, children and teens might not be drawn to exclusive cliques, even in churches. If you feel your child is being shut out or even made to feel unwelcome in your church's children and youth programs, talk with the leader and ask for his or her help. If nothing is or can be done, it may be time to look for a church chosen from your child's point of view. Should your daughter encounter rejection in too many areas of her life, perhaps a talk with a counselor might be helpful. A course in drama, or piano lessons, or some other extracurricular activity might also give her needed confidence.

Again, a word from a wise woman—my mom—who often volunteered to help with church activities: "If you work with young people of any age, please do stress the urgency of making all those who come feel welcome. Some kids have been turned away from the church for years because they were made to feel unwelcome or unimportant in the youth programs of their church. The leader cannot do it all, but perhaps he or she can help with suggestions."

Camps and Mission Trips

Our experience with youth groups has been mostly positive for our children, especially after they went to camp or on a special trip or summer missionary trip with the kids. Zach and Zeke had tremendous experiences with Teen Missions trips to Brazil, Guatemala, and Australia, and I've written of how Scott and I went as teenagers to El Salvador with Teen Missions. Though there was a no-dating policy and we obeyed that rule, we still managed to come home in love. Since dating is in your daughter's future, what a place for her to meet the sort of mate you'd want her to marry someday! I have since had the privilege of speaking at a couple of Boot Camps to hundreds of teens heading out to help a corner of the world, and it never ceases to inspire me.

Just before her junior year, Rachel came down from a backpacking trip with a youth group in Colorado—having matured what seemed like two years in two weeks! She made life-changing spiritual decisions on that mountain, and she had a renewed confidence in her ability, with God's help, to conquer challenging situations. All four of our children loved going to a

Christian camp in east Texas, Jan Kay Ranch—a camp where Scott and I spent many a happy week during our own youth!

Coming to Christ

Before your daughter can put her faith and trust in Christ, she needs to understand who he was, and is, and how much he loves her. It is entirely possible to grow up with all the trappings and motions of Christianity around us—and never fall in love with Jesus himself. We want to help our daughter know and love him, not just turn out to be a good little church-going girl (who ends up in therapy to learn to be more real and authentic).

Begin by sharing with your daughter the most basic of truths: that God is a good, kind Father; that he sent his Son to prove that he, powerful Creator of everything, loves us little human beings down here on planet Earth. Emphasize to her that we don't have to be "good enough" or "smart enough" to deserve this amazing love. All we have to do is believe it, and receive it.

Your daughter may come to a place of receiving this truth gradually as she is surrounded by God's love in your family. Or she may pray to receive Christ's sacrifice for her sins and his all-encompassing love at one very specific point in time. Perhaps it will happen that you will be the one to lead her in this prayer, but it may very well be a Sunday school teacher, or youth director, or a camp counselor. One of our children was led to Christ in this prayer by his little cousin, at about age six, only a year older than he was! Today they both remember that moment.

Making Christ Real to Your Child

One excellent way to understand the sacrificial love of Jesus, in a way children relate to, is to read C. S. Lewis's Chronicles of Narnia with your children. Aslan, the great lion, is a wonderful metaphor of Christ—and one that children, and grown-ups, can easily grasp. Another favorite for my children was a children's version of *Pilgrim's Progress.*

There's a fairly new video series about the life of Christ called the Visual Bible. In *Matthew,* Bruce Marchiano portrays a beautiful version of a Christ who laughed and smiled, cried and hurt. Children have a tremendous need to know that Jesus was real and what he was like. So many of the older movies about Christ make him look like he had all the personality of a lump of dough. A man who changed the world, who inspired the undying love of his companions, was a man full of feelings and personality!

So many well-meaning adults create a picture of Jesus Christ for their children that feels more like a stern, condemning professor, who is busy adding up mistakes, threatening them with punishment for sins, piling on guilt. Even families that use the words "grace" and "mercy" in religious conversation can convey a very different truth by the way they personally respond to God, and pass that belief on to their kids.

Affirming Your Child

A. W. Tozer spoke of "living in the light of God's smile." This is the way we want our daughters to imagine God, their heavenly Father. There is a beautiful blessing in the Old Testament, and I especially like the *Living Bible*'s translation: "May the Lord bless and protect you; may the Lord's face radiate with joy because of you" (Numbers 6:25). As your child goes off to college, off to marry, or simply off to school, perhaps you might send her away with these words of blessing, reminding her of the delight she is to God's heart.

When God spoke aloud about his Son at his baptism, he said very little, but what he said is what every child longs to hear from a parent: "This is my beloved son, in whom I am well pleased." Your children need to hear these words often—from you: "I love you. You bring me such joy and pleasure." If it feels awkward to say these words, you can always write them in a little note or card and leave them on her pillow. She'll cherish these words more than you may ever know.

Psychologists say that the greatest emotional needs of children are to be loved, to belong, and to know their life brings meaning and pleasure to others. In a very few words, God the Father, met all of those needs in his Son. And he did it publicly so others could see and hear how much he valued Jesus.

Publicly praising your daughter is another great way to make her feel loved.

Rave Reviews

How to Study Your Bible for Kids by Kay Arthur and Janna Arndt (Harvest House, 2000)

Now moms who have benefited from Precepts Bible Studies can share the joy of digging for biblical treasure with their daughters.

Just Mom and Me Having Tea (for ages 6–9) by Mary Marray (Harvest House, 2001)

A fun Bible study for mothers and daughters. A keepsake journal filled with lessons to strengthen the special bond between mother and daughter while encouraging her spiritual growth.

The True Princess (for ages 9–12) by Angela Elwell Hunt (Lamplighter, 1999)

A Gold Medallion nominated, beautiful, and highly praised tale about a girl who learns what it means to be a true princess in God's kingdom.

Never, Never, Never Give Up

Someone once said it so well: "There is nothing you can do to make God love you any more, and nothing you can do to make him love you less." When mothers and fathers love their daughters unconditionally, the realization of that will go a long way in helping your daughter view God the same way. This doesn't mean our daughters won't hurt or disappoint us, that they won't need correction and encouragement to make better choices, but it does mean they will always know you love them.

There may be periods in your daughter's life where she tests this love to what feels like your absolute limit. You can be angry. You can cry buckets over her wrong choices. But one thing you cannot do: you cannot stop loving your daughter. It's a Mom Thing and a God Thing.

God, Mom, and Me

Jesus often spoke in parables or demonstrated spiritual truths from nature. He knew that humans think best in visual pictures.

Read Matthew 8:23–27. Think about the scene of Jesus asleep in the boat, with waves billowing around him. Share this picture with your daughter and teach her to mentally climb into the boat and snuggle next to Jesus when she is overcome by the waves of worry.

There's a saying: "Sometimes God calms the storm, sometimes he lets it rage, and calms the child instead." Share this quote with your daughter and ask her what this means to her.

Matthew 6:26, the picture of God caring for the birds, is another strong image for kids who tend toward worry or fear. "Look at the birds of the air; they do not sow or reap or store away in barns, and yet your heavenly Father feeds them. Are you not much more valuable than they?" In fact the entire last half of chapter 6 is wonderful to read through when life is getting us down: it is as worn in my Bible as Psalm 23! For the next week, read Matthew 6:26–34 every day.

At the end of each day, try to ask each other about a time when you were tempted to worry or fret—and you recalled this passage and gave your worries to God instead.

Acknowledgments

Special thanks to Sandy Vander Zicht, both for her incredible patience and kindness as a friend and her amazing talent as an editor. Associate Editor Angela Scheff was a joy to work with as well.

Thanks also to Greg Johnson, my agent, my brother, and my dearest male friend, who has been the wind beneath this writer's wings at times when I wondered if I'd ever get airborne again. Bless you for your prayers and your presence in my life.

My mother, Ruthie, taught me everything I know about raising a daughter, about writing, and about reaching out to Christ when I'm struggling with either one. Her words of wisdom and sparks of humor are sprinkled throughout this book and throughout my life. Thank you.

I named my daughter after my own little sister, Rachel, for an obvious reason: I wanted my daughter to grow up to be as wonderful as her namesake. Thank you, Sis, for your editing expertise and your cheerleading for this project. I'd never have made it through without you.

Also, a huge debt of gratitude to Lynn Morrisey who inspired the chapter about enjoying the classical arts.

Finally, applause to my daughter, Rachel, for allowing me to open the curtains on our mother-daughter triumphs and tangles. I love you, my darling. Thank you for loving me so tenderly in spite of my many mothering mistakes.

For more information about Becky's books and speaking information or to contact her with a comment, visit her website at www.beckyfreeman.com.

WOMENOF**FAITH**ˢᴹ

Women of Faith partners with various Christian
organizations, including
Campus Crusade for Christ International,
Crossings Book Club, Integrity Music,
International Bible Society, Partnerships, Inc.,
and World Vision
to provide spiritual resources for women.

For more information about Women of Faith
or to register for one of our nationwide conferences,
call 1-800-49-FAITH.

www.womenoffaith.com

Dad's Everything Book for Daughters
Practical Ideas for a Quality Relationship
John Trent, Ph.D.

Raising a daughter can be a daunting task for a father, especially when she becomes a teenager. *Dad's Everything Book for Daughters* gives fathers short, practical ideas to build quality relationships with their 8- to 12-year-old daughters so when the turbulent teenage years hit, the relational bond will be so strong that nothing can separate them. Bestselling author, teacher, and speaker John Trent presents short, practical ideas for helping dads make sure their daughters—and their relationship—become strong and well balanced.

This book is filled with ideas on what to talk about and how to go about it. It tells dads how to use teachable moments and how to have Bible studies both he and his daughter will enjoy. It suggests creative ways to bond by doing things she likes to do as well as things he likes to do. It encourages dads and daughters to branch out into new life experiences to create special memories. And it proposes ways they can serve others together. Also included are specific prayers that dads can pray for their daughters.

Softcover: 0-310-24292-4

Pick up a copy today at your favorite bookstore!

Dad's Everything Book for Sons
Practical Ideas for a Quality Relationship
John Trent, Ph.D., and Greg Johnson

AND

Mom's Everything Book for Sons
Practical Ideas for a Quality Relationship
Becky Freeman

The mission is to give dads and moms short, practical ideas to build quality relationships with their 8- to 12-year-old sons so when the turbulent teenage years hit, the relational bond will be so strong that nothing can separate them.

These books are filled with ideas on what to talk about (and how to talk about it); "dates"; retreat fun; how to have Bible studies they both enjoy; how to use teachable moments; creative ways to bond doing things he likes to do, as well as having him do things Dad and Mom like to do; branching out into new life experiences in order to create memories; ways to serve others together; and prayers to pray for sons.

Dad's Everything Book for Sons
Softcover: 0-310-24293-2

Mom's Everything Book for Sons
Softcover: 0-310-24295-9

Pick up a copy today at your favorite bookstore!

We want to hear from you. Please send your comments about this book to us in care of zreview@zondervan.com. Thank you.

ZONDERVAN.com/
AUTHORTRACKER
follow your favorite authors

LaVergne, TN USA
11 June 2010
185812LV00002B/14/P